My Reason & ME

Alison T Smith

Just Alison
Publishing

Just Alison Publishing
Dover, Kent. UK
alison@justalison.me
www.justalison.me

Author's Note: This is my recollection of events and I've related them to the best of my knowledge.

Cover Illustration by Isabel Frewer

Printed and bound in Great Britain by
Orbital Print Ltd, Ashford, Kent

Book Layout © 2016 BookDesignTemplates.com

My Reason & Me / Alison T Smith. -- 1st edition

ISBN 978-0-9955177-1-4

I dedicate this book to my darling son.

Thomas, you have always been the light in my dark times, the energy in my frail times, the hope in my hopeless times, the wind beneath my wings and 'my reason' to keep going whenever I wanted to stop.

I am grateful for the happy, well-behaved child that you were and couldn't be more proud of the kind, gentle, loving man that you have become.

Chapter One

I t was time; I'd waited years for this day, wanting it so badly, more than I'd ever wanted anything before.

I got up on that cold, dark December morning at five o'clock, as I always did, to get ready for my journey to work. Normally, the prospect of the long train journey from our home in Ashford in Kent to my stockbroking job in the City of London filled me with dread. I never wanted to get out of my comfortable, warm bed, especially in the winter months.

This morning was different. I couldn't wait to get up, full of anticipation for what I was about to do. I paused by the bedside for a moment to observe my husband, Tony. Curls of golden hair settled on the back of his neck. He preferred to wear his hair slightly longer than most men did at that time. I always joked that it was to compensate for his deeply receding hairline, although I was fond of his golden locks. This morning, seeing them reminded me of our wedding day three years earlier, when I stood hand in hand with my father, ready to walk down the aisle to my waiting husband-to-be. I noticed then the curls resting on the collar of his suit jacket and still remember it now as if it were yesterday. He looked so smart.

"I think I'm going to cry," I said to my father, Jim. "You're meant to be happy," he replied. I was extremely happy, and proud to become Tony's wife.

As I stood watching him on this morning, I thought how handsome he was; slim and always tanned from the hours spent sun worshipping. He lived for his foreign holidays, sometimes insisting we had two or three a year. Not only did he adore the sun, but also he loved learning about the history of other countries, the people and their cultures. I often wondered how he would feel if we were unable to afford our regular breaks.

I went into the bathroom and found the little box hidden at the back of the bathroom cabinet. I felt sure my feelings were right. There were no signs, apart from the fact that my period was three days late and I was always so regular. I was convinced that a new life, our baby, was growing inside me, and as I was going to my firm's Christmas party that evening I didn't want to risk drinking alcohol if I was pregnant.

My hands trembled with excitement as I did the test and then stood the little white stick up on the toilet cistern, with the indicator windows facing away from me. I couldn't bear to watch as the blue line, or lines, developed. I busied myself by cleaning my teeth. That was all the time the test needed to do its thing. If the test were positive, there would be two blue lines; if not, there would only be one.

I felt nervous. What if my gut feeling was wrong? How would I feel? I'd waited so long. We had actually only been trying for a baby for about a month, but it had taken Tony years to agree to it. He was 32 when we first started living together, and he was 12 years my senior. It took him three years to get around to asking me to marry him, and another three to agree to try for a baby. For me, who had looked forward to having a baby for as long as I could remember, this seemed like a lifetime. Would he be concerned if I fell pregnant so quickly? Maybe he thought it would take some time.

I plucked up the courage to turn the test stick around. There were TWO blue lines. I felt my stomach do a somersault. I was shaking even more now. I felt wonderful, like I was the only woman in the world who had ever been pregnant.

I had already planned that if the test were positive I would tell Tony later that day. We both had our works' Christmas parties that evening, so we'd decided to book into a hotel in London, instead of having the two-hour journey home. I hid the test stick in my bag and when Tony got out of bed I concentrated on acting normal. On a workday in winter at six in the morning, 'normal' didn't include walking around with a permanent grin on my face.

Unfortunately, Tony had awoken with a heavy cold and was plodding around the house with an extremely miserable expression, completely wrapped up in himself and his cold. At least this meant he wouldn't notice my indisputable happiness.

That day at work I felt as though I was walking on air, although I had one very big concern. A work colleague and very good friend and her husband had been trying for a baby for nearly a year, but to no avail. She had confided in me and always kept me informed. There were times when I was her shoulder to cry on. Obviously, I didn't tell her my news that morning as Tony had yet to be told, but I agonised over having to tell her one day soon.

The day seemed to be going really slowly and I couldn't concentrate on my work. I was a Compliance Officer, which meant undertaking surveillance in the various departments of the firm, so I was hardly ever at my own desk. This was a good opportunity to chat to all my friends and keep my mind off my secret.

At lunchtime, I popped out and bought a card and a little toy rabbit from the card shop. I put the pregnancy test stick between the rabbit's paws and wrapped the whole thing in Christmas wrapping paper. On the card I wrote, 'Merry Christmas Daddy! P.S. Mummy says she loves you lots and thank you!'

I was so excited and couldn't wait for that evening. Then the telephone interrupted my thoughts. It was Tony ringing with the news that he felt extremely unwell and had decided not to go to his firm's Christmas party but to head straight home instead. To say I was disappointed would be an understatement. I didn't want to spoil the surprise I had planned so I had to try and convince him to stay over in the hotel without him guessing what I was up to. I suggested that if he felt that bad it would probably be better if he didn't have the long journey home on a draughty, uncomfortable train. He could make the most of going back to a comfortable hotel room, have a warm bath, order room service and settle down in bed in front of the TV. He was obviously sold on the idea because he changed his mind.

My evening out was at the Comedy Store in London, with some colleagues from the Nominee department. I had worked with them prior to getting my position in the Compliance department and we all got on extremely well. The friend trying for a baby was one of them.

When it was time to order our drinks, I ordered an orange juice. Immediately my friend looked me in the eye and asked why I wasn't drinking. I replied flippantly that I didn't feel like drinking alcohol. Now, I was talking to a close friend who I had spent many a drunken night with: a friend who knew me well enough to know that I loved Christmas and the atmosphere of the City and the West End at this time of year, and would throw myself into it wholeheartedly. I knew she knew my secret. Later on, when I visited the ladies room she followed. She just said the words, "You're pregnant, aren't you?"

She showed no malice whatsoever, just delight when I told her that I was. I hugged her and said I was sorry. For some reason I felt I had to. I really felt for her, knowing that she had been trying for so long to have a baby. I can only imagine the disappointment she had felt every month when she realised she wasn't pregnant. I left the restaurant that night with just one thought and hope in my mind... that she would conceive very soon.

Chapter Two

As I made my way in a black cab to the Tower Hotel near Tower Bridge, my thoughts turned to the day I would leave work to have our baby. I always knew that I wouldn't return to work after the baby was born. I wanted a child so much that I had no intention of leaving it for 13 hours a day. I also believed it an important part of my child's education to be given the time and love of a mother and father. I can now appreciate that my mother taught me how to love.

I loved the City not only at this time of year but all year round. My father, Jim, was a Partner at an old and established firm of stockbrokers in the city. He had worked his way up after starting out as a messenger boy and I was extremely proud of him.

Jim was born in 1941 in the East End of London to Arthur and Florence. Florence was only 17 when she gave birth to him, and she and Arthur were married just before the baby came. Sadly, when Jim was only five years old Arthur died from tuberculosis; a year later, Florence died of the same disease. Throughout his childhood, Jim was looked after by nuns and at Dr Barnado's. An aunt finally fostered him and he stayed with her until he got married to my mother, Sue.

Sue and Jim met on the Queen's Coronation Day in 1953,

at a street party in Leytonstone where they both lived. Jim was 11 years old and Sue was 8. They became friends and Jim began to spend a lot of time at Sue's house. Grace, Sue's mother and my grandmother, loved to have a full house and would welcome her children's friends with open arms. As the children grew into teenagers and then adults, they enjoyed many parties at home with Grace.

Jim always took pride in the way he dressed, and even though he was just a messenger in the City when he began work, he wanted his shirts to be ironed well and his collars starched. His foster mother didn't do this well enough for his liking, so after she had ironed them he would take them to Grace for her to iron them 'properly'. Jim has always had great respect for Grace and she was the closest thing to a mother he ever had, welcoming him into her family home. Obviously, Sue would be there and this is when their relationship developed.

I suppose I was destined to work in the City. I looked up to my father and wanted to please him and be who he wanted me to be. I left school when I was 16 and attended the Colchester Institute at Clacton to do a BTEC Diploma in Business Studies. Part of the course involved having some work experience, and my father arranged for me to spend some time with his good friend, Philip, and his colleagues at Quilter Goodison & Co., on the gilt-trading desk. The offices were at Garrard House in Gresham Street; close to the many clothes shops in Cheapside where I would spend my lunch breaks.

I spent two weeks there. The Managing Director at the time was Sir Nicholas Goodison, Chairman of the London

Stock Exchange. I worked with Philip and the other gilt dealers, learning as much as I could about the gilt market. For my exam coursework, I had to complete a project about my work experience. A man called Chris, who was the Director in charge of the Settlements department, asked to see my project when it was completed. He was so impressed with it that he offered me a position in his department when I left college. I was elated; I could go back to college and tell my friends that I had a job in the City of London.

I started work for Quilters, as the firm was often referred to, in August 1984, when I was just 17 years old; my first position was in the UK Dividends department. Chris had told me that he would move me around the various departments so that I could gain experience in every area of the back office. In the eighties, this was how it was.

I made the most of my time at Quilters. I worked hard and played hard. I was commuting from Colchester in Essex, and I would say it took me about a year to get used to the early mornings. The short evenings weren't too much of a problem then because I had my wonderful mother preparing my meals and doing my washing.

I always thought it amusing that my father and I would meet at the front door in the morning and get into the car without a word. We would drive to the station; buy a coffee and a paper; get on the train; read the paper; sleep; wake up at Liverpool St. station; get off the train; walk through the barrier; and kiss each other 'goodbye': only then would we speak. "Have a good day," I'd say.

"What train will you be on this evening?" he would reply.

For the first four years of my career, I moved companies

every year, as this was a good way to gain more experience and obtain an increase in salary. The amount of money I took home was very low to start with and nearly half of it was spent on my train season ticket. I found this frustrating at times, as after paying some keep to my parents, I had very little money left to spend on socialising and clothes. I had always been a classic dresser and, like my father, preferred to be smart, wearing well-cut suits with high heels and handbags to match each of them. I gained so much knowledge and feel very lucky to have spent time at the beginning of my career with the jobbers on the Stock Exchange trading floor, prior to its demise on 27th October 1986 due to the 'Big Bang'.

The 'Big Bang', named because of the increase in market activity expected, was the sudden deregulation of financial markets, including the abolition of fixed commission charges, the distinction between stockjobbers and stockbrokers on the London Stock Exchange, and the introduction of screen-based trading. This was the end of an era, which changed the way my father and all other traditional stockbrokers dealt in stocks and shares. I remember my father telling me that, after the Big Bang, he didn't feel like a stockbroker anymore but a salesman. No longer would he stand among the organised bedlam of the trading floor, using open outcry to communicate. 'Open outcry' is the name of the method of communication they used in the pit (the part of the trading floor where trading took place). It involved shouting and the use of hand signals to transfer information, primarily about buy-and-sell orders.

It was absolutely mesmerising to watch them trade. With

eyes fixed on the jobber, the broker would point a finger at him: this was quickly followed by his holding up a number of fingers to sell; to buy, he would tap his chest and hold up a number of fingers. They generally worked in denominations of 1,000; therefore, three fingers would be 3,000 shares. If the broker didn't want to trade, they would make a horizontal, flat hand movement to the front and out to the side.

The effect of the Big Bang led to significant changes to the structure of the financial markets in London. The changes saw many of the old firms being taken over by large banks, both foreign and domestic, and would lead in subsequent years to further changes to the regulatory environment. These changes would eventually lead to the creation of the Financial Services Authority.

The final company I worked for in the City was NatWest Stockbrokers, which ironically came about due to Fielding Newson-Smith, the traditional stockbroking firm of which my father was a Partner, being taken over by County NatWest. My father became an Associate Director of the institutional side of the bank and I worked for the private client side. When I first started work at NatWest Stockbrokers it was based at Garrard House in Gresham Street, so I had returned to the same building that I'd worked in when I was at Quilters, and this is where I met Tony.

The first time I set eyes on him, I had gone to finalise my employment agreement with Chris, the man who had given me my first job at Quilters. He had become the Director of the Settlements department at NatWest Stockbrokers. At that time in the City, it was often a case of 'It's not what you know, but who you know'. Chris took me over to meet the people I would be working with in the International Settlements department, and Tony was one of them. I was introduced to him; we shook hands and the first thing I noticed about him was his eyes, and that they were full of laughter and fun. He was oh so handsome and, I suppose, if I'm honest, I flirted with him a little! Something clicked inside me but as I was already in a relationship I didn't think any more of it.

I remember very well the week that I started work at NatWest Stockbrokers. I started on Monday 12th October 1987, and on the Friday I didn't make it to work from my home in Southampton because a crippling storm had wreaked havoc; trees lay across roads, trains were cancelled and one-third of England had lost electricity. This later became known as 'The Great Storm' and 'The 1987 Hurricane', as it was the greatest storm to hit England in 300 years. The devastation, which happened in a three-hour period, was swift and dramatic.

Amazingly, I slept through those three hours, with my alarm waking me at 5am, as usual. I walked out of my flat to my car for the drive to the station. What confronted me reminded me of something I had only ever seen on news footage from other countries. It was pitch black, as none of the streetlights were casting their normal amber glow, and I was just about able to make out the long, two-storey block of flats on the opposite corner of our road. I couldn't believe my eyes: the whole of its roof was lying, in one piece, on the ground in front of the flats! Families, with young children still in their nightwear, were milling around in a state of disbelief and, as there were no emergency services there, I assumed it must have not long happened.

"Where are you off to?" a neighbour asked me.

"To get the train to work," I replied.

He laughed and said "I don't think you'll be going anywhere on these roads, let alone a train to London!"

He explained more and, without hesitation, I went home to change out of my suit and heels before giving a hand with the clear-up operation.

The storm, with gusts of up to 122mph recorded in Norfolk, wasn't just responsible for killing at least 22 people in England and France; it was also thought to be, in part, responsible for the single biggest crash the London Stock Exchange had ever experienced.

Many traders and brokers lived in the 'gin-and-Jag belt' of Kent and Sussex, which was the worst hit area. This had an immediate impact on the City, as workers were unable to make it into their offices and the Stock Exchange did not open.

Trouble had been brewing all week on the New York markets, with interest rates being pushed up. People wanted to react by selling their shares, but were unable to do so. All they could do was spend the weekend speculating on how bad Monday's trading would be. It turned out to be worse than anyone could have imagined. By Monday night, the FTSE 100 index had fallen by nearly 11 per cent and £50 billion was wiped off its value. Millions of investors who had bought into the privatisation boom were hit badly, including Jim and his clients.

That day and the day after were the worst two days in the history of the stock market, far exceeding the falls of the 1929 crash and even the turmoil after the collapse of Lehman Brothers. The Great Storm was more than a bout of terrible weather; it became a symbol for the end of an era.

However, it took a while for the full extent of the crash to take effect and as a department we all had a good time. We enjoyed two, three and sometimes four-hour lunches, although we were very conscientious and worked through our lunches and late into the evenings when there was work to be done. We respected our managers and were grateful to have our jobs.

Eventually, Tony and I started to go for a drink at lunchtime without the others. I found Tony extremely easy to talk to and started to open up about my current relationship with Gary.

Chapter Three

Gary was the eldest son of a family that moved into the village where we lived near Colchester. I was about 13 when we started to hang around together with a larger group of friends. We had lived in the same village since leaving our home in London when I was four years old. It was exciting to have a new family to get to know, especially when one of them was a 16-year-old lad. He seemed so much older than me and had his own motorbike.

As a teenager I was never very popular with the boys. I was a real 'plain Jane' and a bit of a tomboy. Unlike my friends I wasn't allowed to wear make-up, so I didn't stand out from the crowd as far as boys were concerned, but Gary seemed to take an interest in me. I was smitten.

We were friends for a couple of years, and eventually when I was about 17 we started to go out together and all our friends knew us as a couple. It was around this time that Gary joined the army and moved away from home. I missed him dreadfully and wrote to him almost every day. I yearned for the times when he came home on leave, and I suppose these times were always fun because we didn't have long enough to get fed up with each other.

We began to dread the times when he had to go back to the barracks and in time we realised that the only way to avoid the 'goodbyes' was to get married and live in married quarters. At just 18 years old I got engaged to Gary. Obviously, my parents were concerned but they gave me their blessing. What else could they do?

We set the date for our wedding as 27th September 1986, which was the following year. It was to be a relatively small wedding with close friends and family. I was always very conscious of my father having to spend a lot of money. To me, a wedding was about a couple getting married because they loved each other, and was not a time to spend massive amounts of money on feeding people that you didn't see from one year to the next or on unnecessary extravagances.

The preparations for the wedding were left pretty much up to my parents and me as Gary was posted to the Falklands for six months and would not be returning until two weeks before the wedding. It was during this time that I started to have doubts about marrying Gary.

I had, by this time, been working in the City of London for nearly two years and had already made my first move from Quilter Goodison to PK Christiania Bank. I was learning a lot about stocks and shares, meeting lots of interesting people, and having a fantastic time. I was going to be moving to Southampton the day after our marriage, to an army house that I had never even seen before. I would be about a four-hour drive away from my family and friends, and as I was used to being surrounded by them I worried that I would be lonely, especially as there would be periods when Gary was away for months at a time.

The commute from door to door would take about two-and-a-half hours, and as there were no trains that ran early enough to get me to work on time I needed to look for another job with a starting time of 9.30 instead of 8.30 in the morning. I was happy working for Christiania Bank and hated the thought of leaving. I was earning significantly more money than Gary was, and if we were to buy a house of our own this would have to continue; especially as Gary didn't appear to be particularly good with money and on occasions got into debt, which I bailed him out of.

One gloriously sunny afternoon in July, while relaxing in our back garden after one of our enjoyable family Sunday lunches, I was thinking how wonderful life was at home in our village surrounded by my family and many friends when my father's words broke into my thoughts. "Isn't it about time we sent out the wedding invitations?" he asked.

"Yes," I replied, in what was obviously not a very convincing tone because he snapped back sharply.

"What's the matter? You don't sound very excited about this wedding!"

At this point, I jumped up and ran into the dining room in tears, with my father following close on my tail. That was the first time for years that I had sat on my father's knee. I told him about my doubts. Doubts that, at the time, I didn't really understand but knew I had to listen to as they had been plaguing me for some time. What about all the money he had spent on the wedding so far? What would people say?

My father was so understanding and kind, explaining that none of that mattered. What mattered was for me not to do something that I might regret for the rest of my life. He made it easy for me to admit that I was doing the wrong thing by marrying Gary, and I felt a great sense of relief. But how would I tell Gary? I still cared about him; I just didn't want to marry him yet. Then, all of sudden I realised I would have to tell him that the wedding was off the next time he called from the Falklands.

It was one of the hardest things I'd ever had to do and felt like a knife to my heart. Gary was due home only two weeks before the wedding so I had no option but to tell him on the phone. There were lots of tears and I tried to soften the blow by telling him that I did want to marry him, just not yet.

When Gary arrived home from the Falklands, I was so happy to see him. He cried on my shoulder and asked me why we couldn't marry that year. I was confused. I felt so good when I was with him. I don't know whether it was the guilt I felt but for some reason I said, "Okay I will marry you, this year." It was the biggest decision of my life, and I made it just like that. I hated to see him hurting and brushed my own feelings aside. We married on a Saturday in the November of the same year; I was just 19. The day after the wedding, I left my family home and moved all of my belongings to married quarters in Southampton.

Within three months I knew I had made a big mistake. I was homesick, commuting for five hours a day and working long hours. Gary worked just five minutes from home and could go home for his lunch. He would finish work at 4.30 in the afternoon, but when I arrived home at 7.30 he would be watching TV, having done nothing. I was the breadwinner and the housekeeper, and I financed almost everything, including his debts.

I had never been one to give up easily and the shame of a divorce was enough to make me look for a solution. I thought that maybe the long hours commuting to London were partly responsible for making me feel low, so I took a job at the Southampton branch of Cobbold Roach & Co., whose head office was in the City. I felt that this would still give me the contact with the City that I craved, just without the long commute.

At first, life felt so much easier, with the 20-minute drive to and from the office meaning I had more time for household chores and a social life. I also had more time to make friends with some of the other army wives, so I didn't feel so lonely. Being Manager of the Client Accounts department was also a step in the right direction in terms of my career. However, none of this changed Gary; in fact, he seemed to become lazier knowing that I was at home more.

After a short time, I started to feel dissatisfied with my job. I missed the buzz of the City and felt that my career was not going to progress in Southampton. I wanted to take the Stock Exchange exams but my managers were not willing to allow me the time to do this or indeed pay for me to do so, as they would have done at a City firm. Unlike when I was in London, I was spending my days with unmotivated people with no ambition. I didn't want to become like them.

I made the decision to go back to work in the City and contacted my friend Chris, who had since moved from Quilter Goodison to NatWest Stockbrokers. Chris was the Director of International Settlements and was looking for someone to join the team. He instantly offered me the job as he knew me, trusted me and had always admired my responsible attitude to work. He became almost like a second father to me, keeping a close, protective eye on me; we developed a strong friendship over the years of my career in the City.

Chapter Four

As time went by, Tony and I shared more and more lunches alone. He was very caring and a good listener. He was a man of few words and didn't say much, but when he did speak he said things worth saying. One day, after listening to me ramble on and on, he asked, "Tell me... exactly why are you with this bloke?" His question rendered me speechless and I just couldn't find one positive reason for being in that relationship.

Eventually, I found the strength to face up to the end of my relationship with Gary. Tony was very much a gentleman in that he wouldn't step on anybody else's toes. I didn't know whether he wanted a relationship with me because he never said or even insinuated that. It didn't matter to me either way. I just knew after talking it through that the relationship I was in wasn't the right one.

After a year of marriage I finally found the courage to tell Gary that I wanted to separate and moved back in with my parents, who were by now living just outside Canterbury, in a country house surrounded by fields: the perfect place for me to recuperate. I felt extremely guilty for doing this to Gary and also felt that I had let my parents down. Should I have fought harder to save our relationship? Did I give up too easily? Or was now the right time to leave? I desperately wanted children, but knew that I didn't want Gary to be the father. I think I had all my answers!

After a very short space of time, literally weeks, I realised that I wanted to be with Tony more and more; he seemed to feel the same. Had he let his guard down now that my relationship with Gary had come to an end? We started to go out for a drink or two together after work most days, as it was becoming harder and harder to leave each other every evening; I somehow felt complete in Tony's company. It was on one of those evenings that Tony pulled me into his arms, as we left the pub, and kissed me passionately on the lips. My stomach did a somersault and for a while afterwards I was speechless. I felt as if I was walking on air on the way to the station and sat on the train dreaming, like a teenager in love.

After that, I visited Tony at his home in Ashford on a few occasions. Although, the times we spent together at his house were always so wonderful, for me, they were tinged with guilt because I had lied to my parents about where I was going. I had not long separated from Gary and I just knew they would disapprove but somehow being with Tony felt so right and I just couldn't fight the need in me.

I suffered numerous journeys to and from Faversham station in the car with my father, trying to pluck up the courage to tell him that I wanted to move into Tony's house in Ashford. The words were always there but something was stopping them from coming out. I was feeling so confused and frustrated, and each day I felt worse. I knew I had to say something soon.

I never felt happier than when I was in Tony's company and I hated saying goodbye to him after work each day. He seemed to have an amazingly calming influence on me, which was just what I needed with the stress of going through a divorce. Gary's solicitor was playing tough and was sending letters to my solicitor requesting that I pay maintenance to Gary for the rest of his life, to keep him in the manner to which he had become accustomed. This was all so upsetting. I had done nothing but bail Gary out of debt the whole time we had been together, and stood to lose money anyway by divorcing him.

Eventually, the moment came when I let my feelings be known, but it wasn't while in the car with my father; it was when I was in the kitchen with my mother and grandmother. My timing after all this was dreadful. My grandfather, Bill, was in hospital after having had major surgery and my grandmother, Grace, was living with us. Did I not have a care for anyone other than myself? The truth was I did, very much so, but I wanted to be with Tony more than anything in the world. He made me feel so special and I loved the fact that he was always happy.

Needless to say my mother and father were very upset, but mostly they were worried. My grandmother was very angry, wondering how I could be so inconsiderate while my grandfather was in hospital. They didn't know this Tony bloke from Adam. He could be a rapist for all they knew, and I was going to live with him.

To be honest, I can't remember a lot of what was said at the time. I remember more strongly the looks on their faces and feeling physically sick at the thought of having let down the most special people in my life. It hurt so badly that I remember wishing I could turn the clock back. I wondered if

Tony was worth ruining everything I held so dear for. For the first time in my life, I felt a huge rift between them and me and it was to take me many years to get over the guilt of this moment.

After a while there was nothing left to say. My mother couldn't bring herself to look at me or even speak to me and I didn't blame her. I decided that the best thing to do was pack my bags and leave, since maybe it would blow over. It took me half an hour to get to Tony's house in Ashford. Although he wasn't expecting me that night, he knew it was only a matter of time. I was crying uncontrollably and he just hugged me without saying a word. He knew how much I was hurting, since he knew how much my family meant to me.

The same week, my father called me at work and suggested that he, Tony and I meet for a drink. For the first time since leaving my parent's house I felt a glimmer of hope that everything would work out fine. I knew that once my parents got to know Tony they would like him and see what a good, kind man he was. I was grateful to my father for extending the olive branch, but felt sure that it was probably my mother's worrying that had prompted him to do so.

We arranged to meet at Balls Brothers in Moorgate and on the way there I felt very apprehensive, not knowing what our reception would be like. When we arrived, I kissed my father on the cheek and Tony shook his hand. My father organised the drinks and immediately barked, "So, you're shagging my daughter then?" He was never one to mince his words.

"No!" replied Tony firmly, not afraid to speak up. "It's much more than that. I happen to love your daughter, Jim."

My father was taken aback by Tony's confidence; he was

used to my previous husband, Gary, almost shying away from him when he spoke. It was obvious that my father was impressed by the fact that this man 'had balls', as he would say.

Even so, my father continued to give Tony a bit of a grilling for a while. Tony was 32 and I was only 20; to my father, this was an unreasonable age gap and he was clearly concerned about Tony's motives. On the plus side, there was no ex-wife or children. Tony appreciated and understood my father's worries and didn't take any of his comments to heart or react to them. I think this impressed my father even more.

As the three of us continued to chat, it became apparent that my father and Tony had a mutual interest in fishing. Tony had been a keen course fisherman since he was a child and my father had fished in the canals of London since he was five years old, later fishing for the Stock Exchange's own club. I was happy to see them chatting easily about their lives and was relieved that they seemed to have 'hit it off', as my father's opinion was everything to me.

After a while the conversation inevitably got around to football, with my father being a staunch West Ham supporter and Tony a fan of Arsenal. "Well you can forget about ever marryin' my daughter if you're a Gunners man!" my father said with a smile.

"We'll see about that!" replied Tony.

As we all left the bar, my father shook Tony's hand again, saying: "You betta' look after my daughter! You don't, and your life won't be worf livin'!"

"Oh I will, don't worry," Tony replied. "It was good to meet you, bye Jim."

"Bye Dad!" I chipped in.

I felt like I was walking on air as Tony and I walked back to our office in Gresham Street. I put my arms around Tony and squeezed him tight, giving him a long, hard, lingering kiss on his cheek. "I love you, Tone," I said. "You handled that brilliantly and I'm so proud of you!"

"Ah it was a piece-a'-piss!" he joked. "'E's alright!"

I will never know what my father told my mother when he returned home, but that evening she rang to ask Tony and me to lunch the following Sunday. Talk about unconditional love. Of course, we accepted the invitation with hope and gladness. From the moment Sue and Tony set eyes on each other, it was obvious that their relationship would be a special one.

Chapter Five

So there I was, six years later, travelling to meet my knight in shining armour at the Tower Hotel, to tell him the wonderful news: a new beginning in our relationship.

When I got to our room I fully expected to see Tony curled up in bed and most likely fast asleep, but he wasn't there. I guessed that he had decided to go to the party after all. I was glad as it obviously meant he was feeling better. I had a warm bath, slipped on the fluffy white bathrobe provided by the hotel and made myself a cup of tea. I sat by the window, impatient and excitedly waiting for Tony to arrive while watching boats of partying people go by on the River Thames. I love the sight of Tower Bridge lit up at night, with its reflection on the river. To this day, whenever I see it I remember our special night.

Tony rolled in about an hour later. He was extremely merry with drink and made me laugh with his antics as usual. He had had a good evening after all and the best was yet to come. I let him get into bed before removing my robe and snuggling up to his warm, slender body. I gave him a long, lingering kiss, and then told him in a soft, husky voice, "I've got something for you!"

"Oh yes?" he replied, with a cheeky grin.

I rolled over and took the wrapped 'gift' from the bedside table drawer. He looked at me curiously, wondering why I was giving him a Christmas present now. He opened the present first, not noticing the pregnancy test stick, and then he read the card. His face was a picture; I needn't have worried that he would think it too soon. He threw the rabbit up in the air and yelled, "I'm gonna be a daddy!"

He didn't stop hugging and kissing me. I felt elated and so special. I told him about that morning and the rest of my day. Then he looked me in the eyes and said, "How about having a go at making it twins?" This was a typical Tony comment.

We decided to tell our families at Christmas; although it was still early days, I knew that if anything unfortunate were to happen I would need my family to know anyway, to help me through it. My family has always been a huge support to me in my times of need.

We told Hazel and Terry, Tony's parents, the day before Christmas Eve. Hazel had given up hope of having grandchildren, as she felt Tony was getting too old at nearly 40. We gave her a present of baby wool and a knitting pattern. She cried tears of happiness and Terry looked chuffed to bits. We had made their Christmas complete.

As we were spending Christmas with my parents, we told them, along with my brother, sister, brother-in-law, and niece and nephew, our news on Christmas Eve. I think it was my niece, Jessica, who changed Tony's view of children. Before she came along he hadn't had much to do with babies and his view was that they were just eating, crying and pooping machines. As he spent more time with Jessica, he realised that they are actually funny, interesting little beings.

I think that's when he became sold on the idea of us starting a family.

Sue, knowing her daughter better than she knew herself, somehow guessed before the news was even shared. Everybody was ecstatic; they knew how long I had wanted a child. This was going to be a fantastic Christmas. On Christmas morning, there was huge excitement in the household, with my sister's children, Jessica and Nicholas, opening their presents and playing with their toys. It was the perfect Christmas morning for Tony and me, imagining our future Christmases with our child (and hopefully children) in the years to follow.

The women got on with preparing the festive feast while the men occupied the children, with my brother, James, making regular trips to the kitchen to ask when dinner would be ready. Lunch was finally served and we sat down to a marathon session at the table.

After I had stuffed myself so full that I could hardly move, I made a trip to the toilet before tackling the washing up with the others. My heart sank and tears welled up in my eyes when I discovered that I was losing blood. I cried out for Tony, who came running. When he realised what was happening, he called my mother and the three of us were squashed inside my parent's downstairs toilet, with my mother consoling me the best she could. She suggested I rest with my feet up for the rest of the day. I felt devastated and was frightened that I was going to lose the baby I had yearned for for so long. Tony was by my side most of the day; at times his face looked as though it would crumble. I thought the worst.

My sister, Tina, who had had two healthy children, looked extremely concerned but hugged me and told me she was sure everything would be okay. Tina is only two years older than I am, but has always felt older. Ever since I had been a young child, she had always protected me. She was very much the 'mother hen'. When she left school she trained as an NNEB Nursery Nurse and therefore knew a lot about pregnancy and childbirth. She told me that, sometimes, pregnant women lose some blood around the time that their period would have been due. For some reason this didn't console me; I was still convinced that I was going to lose our baby. All those years that I had wanted a child, never once did it enter my mind that I might not be able to have one.

We had planned to visit Hazel and Terry again on Boxing Day, so we drove to their house and gently told them what had happened. They were fantastic. Hazel sat me on the sofa and told me not to move, just rest. She cooked a lovely dinner and we had an enjoyable day.

Even though the bleeding had stopped, I decided to call the doctor just to check that I was doing the right thing. I was due back to work the following day and wasn't sure whether I should make that long journey, which involved a lot of walking to and from stations. The doctor came out to see me and confirmed that rest was the best option. He explained that if I were going to miscarry it would be for all the right reasons; he also said that bleeding does sometimes occur around this time due to the acidic environment of the womb. I felt 80% better. I was advised to take the rest of the week off work.

Chapter Six

Well, we survived the trauma of very early pregnancy and my baby grew and grew. I felt absolutely great during the pregnancy, other than slight nausea first thing in the morning and sometimes in the evening. Tony would bring me a cup of tea and two ginger biscuits before I got out of bed each morning. This seemed to help tremendously, allowing me to make the journey to work without running back and forth to the toilets on the train for fear of being sick. I had all the normal checks and everything was fine. Tony came with me for the scan and we watched with glee as the baby kicked both legs out and moved its hands around. I said to Tony, "Look it's waving at us."

"Nah! That's not a wave, that's a 'V' sign!" he replied. Trust him!

When I had reached the 15-week point, I received the most fantastic news. The friend that had been trying for a baby for over a year was pregnant! Her baby was due in October and mine on 20th August. It was great to swap stories of our pregnancies.

At 27 weeks into my pregnancy, it was Tony's 40th birthday. As I was leaving full-time employment, I knew it would probably be a while before I was able to really treat him again so I booked a surprise weekend trip to Paris. We were to fly out on the Friday morning, which was his actual birthday. I made secret arrangements with his firm, telling them he wouldn't be at work that day, and booked the tickets. On the morning of his birthday I set the alarm for our normal time of rising for work so that he wasn't suspicious. I wished him 'happy birthday' with a big kiss and gave him a card; inside, I had placed the tickets for our trip.

He was flabbergasted that I had managed to keep it a secret and asked when we were going. "We fly at 10am so get your skates on," I replied.

Of course I got all the questions, like "What about work?" and "Is it alright for you to fly in your state?"

He was amazed that so many people seemed to know but hadn't let on. It wasn't until we got to the airport and were checking in that it all finally sunk in. Tony gave me a huge hug and thanked me again. For him, this was a wonderful present, as he loved travelling. He didn't even seem fazed that he wouldn't be at home to watch the FA Cup Final the following day; luckily for me, it was between Everton and Manchester and didn't involve the Gunners! I'm not sure I would have been as popular then! I felt really satisfied and got so much joy from seeing the excitement on his face. Our time in Paris was very special: our last break on our own before the baby came.

At 33 weeks' pregnant I was to leave work. My birthday was on the Thursday of that week and I left NatWest Stockbrokers on the Friday. On my birthday, I took a few of my girlfriends to our favourite wine bar, the Aldgate Colony, and the day after I invited just about everyone I knew, from past jobs and present, to The White Swan in Alie Street, just opposite our offices. The place was absolutely jam-packed with my friends and thankfully it was a scorcher of a day so everyone was able to spill out onto the pavement. This was it; after 11 years spent working in the City, of which just over seven were at NatWest Stockbrokers, I was leaving. I felt quite emotional and at the same time so excited to think of what lay ahead.

I had driven into work that day, as Tony and I were going to stay at Tina and Keith's house in Colchester that weekend. It proved a sensible decision to take the car in, as I was given so many lovely gifts, one being a car seat for our baby; I would never have managed everything on the train, even with Tony's help!

I was exhausted when we arrived at my sister's house. I had been suffering with swollen ankles for the previous couple of weeks, and the blistering heat and long commute every day hadn't helped. On this day, I had also stood for about five hours in a hot and crowded pub, so that evening was no exception. Tina settled me onto the sofa with cushions to raise my feet higher than the rest of my body.

I was very much relieved to have finally left work as I had been finding the journey far too tiring. The heat had made my feet and ankles swell to the extent that it was quite uncomfortable to walk and even fit into any of my shoes. It was at this time that the building work relating to the Channel Tunnel was taking place at Ashford train station and we had to park what seemed like miles away from the station each day.

So this was it; there were just seven weeks until the baby

was due. I had so much to do before I was organised, but I knew I was going to enjoy every moment of the preparations. At last I could concentrate on our forthcoming happy event and not work. For the first time since I was 17, I enjoyed not having to get up at 5am to travel to London. I didn't realise how stressful it was until I stopped doing it. I loved having the time to prepare the nursery, make curtains for the kitchen, and do all those jobs around the house that I just didn't have time for when I was away for such long hours.

Tony didn't drive, but as it was summer he was happy to walk to the station to give me some extra time in bed in the morning. By that stage, I was quite heavily pregnant and wasn't having a good, continuous sleep at night. Every day, I looked forward to fetching Tony home from the station and watching the pleasure on his face as I told him about my day and what I had achieved in preparation for our new arrival. As we relaxed watching TV each evening, the baby would be really active and we would have so much fun trying to guess which part of its body we could feel. Tony would tap my bump gently and say, "'allo Daddy 'ere".

Even though he was born in Cornwall and lived all his life in Kent, he had more of a cockney accent than I did. It was sometimes hard to believe that he wasn't from East London like me. I often thought that maybe it had something to do with the fact that he started work in London at the age of 15 and mixed with a lot of Londoners.

Tony took a few days off work in the July to go and watch the test cricket at Canterbury. Just before he left for the train, the postman brought the mail. There was a large white envelope addressed to us both in what looked like Tony's mother's handwriting. It looked as if it could be a card. We looked at each other and laughed in realisation of what we'd done. We must have been so wrapped up with thoughts of our impending arrival that we had BOTH forgotten our wedding anniversary. We found this highly amusing and wondered how differently we would have felt if only one of us had forgotten.

Chapter Seven

Luckily, I felt the nesting instinct quite strongly and got organised fairly quickly because, just over three weeks after leaving work, I was admitted to hospital. My blood pressure was very high and I had pitting oedema and protein in my urine. The midwife was concerned, as these are all symptoms of a condition called pre-eclampsia, which can be dangerous to mother and baby. By this time I was 36 weeks into the pregnancy. My blood pressure and the baby were monitored regularly throughout the day, and in the beginning I enjoyed my time in hospital.

I made friends with other mums-to-be, relaxed totally and spent my days doing cross-stitch and waiting for the next meal or drink to be brought to my bed. This was interspersed with the midwife bringing the heart monitor machine to my bedside. They were grateful that, by this time, I had become quite adept at finding the baby's heartbeat and attaching the monitor to the right place myself.

It was great not having to think about shopping, cooking and housework while I was in hospital, but I did miss Tony and our special times in the evening with my bump, and cuddling up to him in bed at night. I worried about him having a long day at work, getting home from London at 7pm and then walking to the hospital to visit me, although seeing him was always the highlight of my day.

At one point during my stay, I had a scare when the doctors thought I had a deep vein thrombosis and whisked me off for a scan. This turned out to be a very funny experience and I continued to tell the tale for some years after!

As I was supposed to be having complete bed rest, I was delivered in a wheelchair to the doctor who was to undertake the Doppler ultrasound scan. He was the most handsome man ever, about my age and very fit! Admittedly, I may have been seeing him through rose-tinted glasses at the time, due to the fact that I had not been at home for well over a week and therefore had not had the loving attention of my husband!

The doctor helped me up onto the couch, which was no simple task for the poor man, as I was very heavily pregnant and, shall we say, the ginger biscuits at the beginning of my pregnancy had taken their toll on my weight. It isn't particularly comfortable or easy to lie flat in that condition, so he asked me to sit up on the edge of the couch facing him. He pulled a chair up, which he sat on, and then took my leg and placed my foot between his legs... surprisingly close to his groin area!

As I said, this man was an absolute Adonis and I felt the heat rising from his soft, warm groin area all the way up my leg to my face, where I flushed profusely. I was scared to even wiggle my toes! He gently smoothed some cold gel on the whole of my leg, which did go a long way to calming, I mean cooling, me down. Then, he ran his implement up and down the length of my leg, from ankle to groin...

It turned out not to be deep vein thrombosis, but it was safer to be sure and, apart from that, the whole experience made my week in hospital so worthwhile! However, after two weeks in hospital, I started to become stir crazy. The doctors allowed me home for a few days on the understanding that I rested and returned to the antenatal clinic at the hospital the following Wednesday. It was bliss to have a bath and get into my own bed with Tony. I did as I was told and rested, although I found it much harder with the temptations of my nesting instincts to clean the house from top to bottom, especially as I was feeling so well.

On the Wednesday, my mother took me to the clinic. I was advised by the midwife to take my packed bags with me just in case I was admitted. I only had 13 days to go until my due date and hoped that they would take me in and induce me. My prayers were answered and they did, on account of my blood pressure being dangerously high. I was induced first thing on Thursday morning. Tony took the day off work to be at the hospital, and my mother was there too.

Right from the very beginning of my pregnancy, Tony didn't want to be at the birth. He had a real phobia of hospitals and didn't feel he could be there, so I asked my mother to be with me instead. I didn't want to be alone. My mother felt honoured as she had always dreamt of being present at a birth and for it to be her grandchild's made it even more special. It would appear, though, that all the time Tony spent with me in the hospital prior to the birth cured his phobia because he changed his mind.

After the midwife had done her bit, Tony, my mother and I played scrabble while we waited for my contractions to start.

They didn't, but I did have a terrible ache in my back and found it very difficult to get comfortable. Even though I had been told to rest because of my blood pressure, I found it much more comfortable to take little walks around the corridors with my mother or Tony.

Later in the day, I was having to breathe deeply through the back pain and realised that this was obviously the way I was going to experience my contractions. I was strapped to a monitor so that the midwives could observe the contractions, which they did very rarely. I was happy, though, knowing that things were moving along nicely.

In the bed next to mine, a woman who was in the first stages of labour was screaming and yelling and making a real fuss. She had three midwives regularly checking her over and telling her it wasn't yet time for her to move to the delivery suite. With all the commotion, they obviously forgot about me because a while later one came over casually and said, "Right let's see how things are going here." I don't think she was expecting much because I wasn't making a fuss, but she gasped and said "Oh, my dear, I think it's time we got you to the delivery room!"

My contractions were about four minutes apart, but I insisted that I have a bath first. My mother took me into the bathroom and helped me in the bath. It was sheer bliss. The warmth of the water made the pain disappear and I just wanted to stay in there forever, but my mother wasn't having any of it. She gently tried to hurry me, helping me get back into my nightdress. Just as I put on my clean underwear I felt a warm gush between my legs as my waters broke. I kept telling my mother to make sure she told a nurse in case another lady slipped on the puddle on the floor.

It was only a matter of seconds until the pain hit me with a vengeance. A midwife brought a wheelchair around and wheeled me to the labour ward, with my mother and Tony in hot pursuit. By then, it was about eight o'clock in the evening.

Then, almost instantly I needed pain relief, gas and air; as much as possible, please! That did the trick and helped me through the contractions. A little later the midwife suggested that I have an epidural as the baby was in a bit of distress and my blood pressure was dangerously high. Even though I didn't feel the need for more pain relief I said, "Yes, of course, you do what you need to do."

I was in their hands; I knew they knew what was best for my baby and me. Within about five minutes though, I was asking impatiently where my epidural was! After the epidural was administered, I slept like a baby for about five hours.

Chapter Eight

I awoke to see a cosily lit room and Tony sound asleep in a comfortable chair in the corner. I could tell that my mother was just dozing, completely alert to what was going on in the room: my dear mother, always concerned for me before herself.

As requested, my mother informed the midwife when I awoke so that I could be examined. My cervix was completely dilated; it was time to push. Unfortunately, my contractions died away to nothing, which meant forceps had to be used to pull the baby out and I would have to be cut slightly. The midwife, knowing how Tony felt about hospitals and hospital procedures, suggested he might like to move to the room next door, so as not to witness the next part; he agreed without question not wanting to see any blood and gore!

I needed to have a top up of the epidural so that the doctor could cut without causing me pain, which meant I was numb and would be unable to feel any contractions. The midwife had to tell me when to push, as I couldn't feel the natural urge and at this point there were no contractions. I had never before put so much effort into anything as I did that night. I pushed with all my body, mind and soul. After about two or three pushes I felt immense relief as my baby was placed on my stomach at 3.53am. The first sight I had of my baby was his swollen, red testicles. I was left in no doubt as to his gender and thought of how proud Tony would be of his son's 'tackle'. It's a man thing!

Any woman who has had a baby will know how I felt at that moment. It is a feeling I still find hard to sum up with words. I often wish I could have bottled it to enable me to relive that time, again and again. My first words were, "Daddy will be pleased, he's got a son, Thomas James, or T.J."

Thomas has never really been called T.J. It's just something Tony and I joked about when we were trying to decide on names. We found it very hard to agree on boys' names. If we had a boy I wanted to call him Anthony James, after Tony and my father, but Tony didn't agree. He wanted to name him after his grandfather, Tom, who he had been extremely close to. With Thomas also being Tony's middle name, we finally settled on this and my father's name.

I lay watching my newborn baby boy with an immense feeling of pride, but there was one thing missing, my husband. He was in the room next door and wasn't able to share in my joy at that time. The doctor took Thomas to Tony, and to this day I am sad that I didn't see the look on Tony's face as he saw our son for the first time, although there were to be many more special moments to come, which I will always cherish. The pride I felt has stayed with me from that day to this and the love I have for Thomas has grown deeper with the passing years.

I needed to have some stitches to repair the cut that was made for the forceps delivery. The doctor, a black African man with a big, bright, white-toothed smile, put my feet up in stirrups as I lay on the bed. I remember saying to him as I looked through my legs at his happy face, "What'ya doing down there, cross-stitch? Put a couple of extra stitches in will you?"

I was elated and not in any pain whatsoever, which is a huge relief after giving birth. By about nine o'clock that morning, I was back on the ward with my new baby by my side. Thomas slept soundly for quite a few hours; as for me, I was far too excited and overjoyed to even think of sleeping. I had lost quite a lot of blood and was unable to sit up without feeling extremely lightheaded and faint, so I stayed on my side, observing the perfect form of my baby. His head was a bit battered and bruised as a result of the forceps and he looked as though he had fought 10 rounds in a boxing ring, but he was perfect!

Tony and my mother left the hospital once I had returned to the ward. They were in desperate need of sleep and a shower, having been up all night with me. My mother always talks of the time when, as they were leaving the ward, Tony put his arm around her shoulders and said, "Well, we did it didn't we?" Then he ran, at full speed, along the corridor, jumped and clicked his heels to one side.

Later that day, while my mother was in the shower, Tony went running up the stairs calling to her. She worried that he was about to burst into the bathroom and catch her naked, he seemed so excited. He had just discovered from his mother that that day was the anniversary of his granddad Tom's death. This, for him, was a happy coincidence, as he loved Tom dearly and missed him terribly. Now it seemed even more appropriate that Tom's great-grandson was named after him.

Later in the afternoon, I was able to sit up gradually, eat some Weetabix with refreshingly cold milk, and then go for a slow walk. As I walked gingerly down the corridor, like a cowboy who had been on his horse for days, the doctor who had stitched me up was walking towards me. He gave me one of his huge grins and said, "Aha, not so cocky now are we?"

"I'll get you at playtime!" I told him.

My first visitor of the day was my neighbour Lorraine. I hadn't known Lorraine long at this time, even though she, her husband Dennis, and her daughter Laura only lived opposite us. Prior to leaving work, my evenings and weekends were very much taken up with cooking, cleaning, washing, DIY and sleeping; therefore, I didn't get to meet the people I lived near. Quite soon Lorraine and I became good friends. She came across as a happy, down-to-earth and honest person, and that appealed to me. Thomas and I spent many enjoyable hours with Lorraine and her daughter. Laura and Thomas used to pretend they were brother and sister and played together really well, despite the age gap of about three years.

My first night with Thomas is one I will remember forever. It was a special time for getting to know my baby and learning together. That night, we learnt how to breastfeed. It took quite a few attempts but we got there in the end. Thomas had, unlike me, caught up with his sleep during the day and didn't want to sleep; the only thing that stopped his crying was being cuddled by me. This little person wanted me and me only! The feelings I had were too hard to resist and I just wanted to hold my baby in my arms to make him feel safe. At one point in the night I remember a nurse coming in and tucking the sheet tightly around us both so that Thomas wouldn't fall out of bed. I slept quite soundly for the rest of the night with my lips touching his soft, silky head.

The next morning, as I was stirring from my sleep, it was almost as if I had forgotten where I was and what had happened the day before; the fact that I was now a mum. I opened my eyes to see Thomas's big, wide-awake eyes staring back at me, and the memories of the day before came flooding back. As I told Tony this later that morning, his eyes filled with tears. I had never before seen him moved to tears like that and I loved him more than ever. That was to be the first of many times I saw tears in Tony's eyes when it came to our darling son. Thomas changed Tony and the way he behaved. It was a wonderful sight to behold.

The months to follow were among the happiest I had ever spent with Tony. Thomas was a happy and contented baby who never minded me lifting him out of his cot and dressing him in his snowsuit on freezing winter mornings at 6am to take 'Daddy' to the station.

We managed to afford a holiday to Lanzarote in the October after Thomas's first birthday. For Tony, I think this was the 'piece de resistance'; not only could he have this wonderful child, he could still have holidays abroad. We had a fantastic time, and as usual Thomas was as 'good as gold'. We spent most of our days around the pool or on the beach, and then in the evenings we would give Thomas his dinner, tuck him up in his pushchair, and walk to a restaurant where Tony and I would have our meal.

Sometimes we would be at the table for two hours or more and Thomas would sit happily in his pushchair without a fuss. He would have us, and the rest of the people in the restaurant, in fits of laughter with his antics. We often received compliments on the way he behaved and how happy he was. We felt extremely proud of our little boy and were amazed that even teenage boys would comment on how cute he was. Tony and I felt like the luckiest, happiest people alive.

Thomas filled our days with so much joy, and life was absolutely wonderful for us. I had everything I had ever wanted... except maybe a brother or sister for our little boy! Tony and I decided to try for another child when Thomas reached two years old.

Chapter Nine

Two months after our holiday, it was Christmas and Tony, Thomas and I were going to Wales, along with the rest of my family, to spend Christmas with my father.

My father had agreed to look after a pub for a friend who had lost his wife to cancer. The friend, George, wasn't sure whether he wanted to keep the pub or sell it, so he went away for a while to take time to decide. My father agreed to take over the management of the pub for three years, but as my brother, James, was in the process of taking his GCSE exams, my mother had to stay at home in Canterbury to look after him. She thought this would be an ideal opportunity for my father, as he had retired from stockbroking at just 47 years old and always seemed to be at a loss for something to do. At 54 years old he was still young at heart and physically fit, so this seemed like the perfect opportunity. My father had always wanted to run a pub and was perfect landlord material and she knew he would have a great time.

I think my mother also hoped that 'absence would make the heart grow fonder'. After 34 years of marriage, their relationship was strained and not as happy as it could be. She decided that she and James would make the journey to the Wye Valley as often as they could to see him, maybe every other weekend. With my father getting home every so often as well, it should have meant the periods apart weren't too long.

Tony, Thomas and I drove down in our car on Christmas Eve, with my grandparents, Grace and Bill, following behind in their car. The journey to the pub varied considerably each time we went. Sometimes we would make it in three hours, but at other times it would take six. Thomas was only 16 months old but was very happy and well behaved on long journeys; he caused us no problems at all.

As Tony had been at work that day and hadn't had a meal, we decided to travel on the back roads and stop for something to eat at The Black Swan in Ockham, which was en route. We also thought it would be pleasant to spend some time with my grandparents before we reached the 'chaos' of the pub.

We had an enjoyable meal and a laugh as we always did when Tony and Bill got together. It was hard to believe that Grace and Bill were in their mid-seventies because they were so full of life, laughing and joking and telling tales of their lives. I have always been extremely proud of them both. Bill was a Normandy and Arnhem war veteran who fought for our country and knew what it was to suffer. Grace, who was left alone when Bill was fighting, worked hard all her life and also knew what suffering was.

Tony was relieved that it was the holiday period at last. He said that he felt absolutely shattered, which I understood only too well, having worked in the City. At Christmas, there were so many dinners and drinks parties to go to; along with normal workloads it could be a very tiring time. He was relieved when we finally arrived at the pub in a village not far from Chepstow. There already to greet us were my parents, my brother, James, my sister, Tina, and her family, who had arrived earlier in the day. Over the previous months, we had also got to know the locals, so it was great to see them all again. We took our luggage up to our rooms, Tina and I got the children to bed and then we adults started to get into the Christmas spirit, metaphorically speaking!

My father made a great landlord, just as we always thought he would. He has always been a party animal and loves being with different people. Since it was Christmas Eve, the pub was extremely lively and buzzing that night, and although Tony was quiet, compared to my father, he loved meeting and speaking to different people. He was helping out behind the bar, serving drinks and being the perfect host. The locals loved him and as usual he was making everyone laugh. We all became quite merry and had a fantastic evening. It was one of the best Christmas Eves I'd ever had, surrounded by my whole family.

Tina and I wore Santa hats and were dancing around behind the bar, making Tony laugh. We were doing our 'shu-bup' bit, like the backing singers of a band, and having a blast. My sister and I have always been very close. Of course we squabbled, as children do, when we were younger, but we always protected each other if the need arose. When I was a teenager it was always Tina that I discussed puberty problems with, as I was too embarrassed to go to my mother, goodness knows why as in later years I could tell her everything. As we were getting older, that love was growing and felt very different to when we were kids. As for my 'little' brother, James, he is one of the most wonderful things that happened to our family. He made a very dramatic and shaky arrival into the world when Tina and I were in our teens. Even though my mother was classed as geriatric on all her doctor's notes, the pregnancy went well, until the end when there were complications. After haemorrhaging badly at home one Sunday evening, she was rushed to hospital, where she remained for some time until nearer the baby's due date.

Eventually, the pregnancy was induced but again there were complications. My mother suffered a placental abruption, whereby the placental lining separates from the uterus of the mother prior to delivery. Thankfully, a nurse was passing at the time and acted fast. She gathered up the placenta and held it back in place while an emergency caesarean was undertaken.

When my father arrived at the hospital, he was told that he had a son and that if he survived there would be a 90% chance of him suffering brain damage, due to the lack of oxygen endured. He was also told that my mother was in a critical condition and that she too could lose her life. When my father finally got home from the hospital he looked exhausted, to say the least. None of us slept a wink that night from worry.

Thankfully, my mother and our little brother turned out to be fighters. James didn't suffer any form of brain damage and became a wonderfully happy addition to our family. He takes after my father in a lot of ways, being confident, witty and very charming, but he also has many of my mother's wonderful traits; he is sensitive, loving and caring. He was a great support to my mother while my father was away at the pub. On this particular evening James was on top form, making everyone laugh with his antics, jokes and impressions.

I remember at one point sitting on my brother-in-law Keith's knee and telling him how much I loved him. Keith has always been special to our family. He is more like a brother to me than a brother-in-law. Tina started going out with him when she was 17 years old, but we had known him and his family for years before that, and I went to primary school with his brother, Darren. Keith began to live with us when his mother and father moved to another village. It was easier for Keith to travel from our house to his work as a carpenter and joiner. At one stage we even had his sister living with us. That's how my parents were: our home was open to anyone. Parties and get-togethers were common occurrences. James, at the time, was only about two years old, so Keith is like a real brother to him and they are very close.

Although we had had some fantastic times together as a family, this particular Christmas Eve was different. It's not just now when I think back on it; I actually felt it at the time. It was a special evening when we were all really together as a family, and I felt so wonderfully happy and content. I had everything I wanted and needed.

Chapter Ten

Thomas didn't wake up until eight o'clock on Christmas morning. He was still young and didn't yet understand that Father Christmas had visited him in the night! I was glad of the lie in, as we hadn't got to bed until three in the morning.

As always, he lay in his cot cooing and chattering and for a while I cuddled up to Tony, who was still very much in the land of nod. I remembered what he had said the day before about being tired and not to wake him too early. So I slipped out of bed, lifted Thomas from his cot, gave him a long cuddle and left the room to join the rest of the family. My niece and nephew were opening their presents and were full of excitement. I decided to give Thomas a couple of small presents to open but to wait until Tony got up before letting him open the rest.

I went to wake Tony at about 11 o'clock. There was plenty of time, as our dinner wouldn't be until after the pub had closed at about three o'clock. Tony was still sleeping soundly and was very difficult to rouse. I asked him if he wanted to get up to watch Thomas open the rest of his presents. He mumbled something along the lines of "Yeah, in a minute."

So I busied myself, washing and dressing Thomas and tidying the room. I thought it would do no harm to leave

Tony to sleep for another half an hour or so, while I went for a shower, so I took Thomas into the other room to play with his cousins.

While I got dressed, I called out to Tony, again saying, "Come on Tony, don't you want to see your son open his presents?" By this time I was starting to get a bit miffed.

I knew he was tired but this was getting beyond a joke. I made some snide comment and left the room, slamming the door behind me. I went down to the bar to have a drink with some of the locals. People were asking where Tony was and I explained that he was still lazing in bed and that I wasn't very happy that he hadn't got up to see Thomas open his presents. After a while my annoyance subsided and I had a laugh with everyone.

Just after one o'clock, when Tony still hadn't surfaced, I decided to go upstairs and jump on him. When I got to him, I noticed that he was soaked in sweat and still out for the count. I began to think he must have the flu or something similar. After all, at that time of year it was quite common and he had had a number of long, tiring days. I started to feel slightly guilty for having a moan about him. I stroked the damp hair from his forehead and spoke softly to him, asking if he felt unwell. This time he started to talk to me, but the words he was saying didn't make any sense.

He said things like, "Oi mate 'ave you paid for that drink?" and "That'll be £5.20 please, mate."

I laughed, thinking that he was messing around as usual, but as I asked him more questions I realised he wasn't. He seemed delirious and not fully awake. I became frightened as he was acting very strangely. I began to get upset and tried to wake him. When he didn't wake up, I left the room and ran to fetch somebody. I felt as though I flew down the four flights of stairs, my feet hardly touching the ground. I burst into the bar and the first people I saw were my father and my brother-in-law, Keith. I shouted through my tears, "Come quick, something isn't right with Tony. He's saying funny things and he won't wake up."

When we reached his bedside my father tried to rouse him, "Tone, come on mate, you gonna get up? Ya son wants to open his pressies."

I could tell my father was trying to act normal, for me I suppose. He was my 'daddy', the strong, brave man who had always sorted out my problems since I was a child; more than ever before, I wanted him to sort this one.

When Tony did finally wake up, the first thing I noticed was that his eyes were different. The laughter had gone; the laughter, which I noticed in his eyes when I first met him and which was, more often than not, there in all of the nine years that I had known him, had gone. He looked at me as if he didn't know me, or even where he was.

Our first thought was that he had been asleep for a long time and had not had any fluids. Although he had drunk alcohol the previous evening, it was nowhere near as much as he would have done if he hadn't been serving behind the bar. I had seen him a lot worse for wear on alcohol before. I went to the sink in the corner of our room to fetch him a drink of water and noticed that he had been sick. It hadn't been there when I had washed Thomas earlier, so it had obviously happened since I had been trying to wake him. When I asked him, he said that he thought he had been sick earlier but wasn't too sure.

My father commented that Tony might feel better if he had a shower and drank some water and a cup of weak, sweet tea, so we encouraged him to get out of bed. This proved extremely difficult, as he was so sleepy. My father, Keith and I all helped him down the flight of stairs to the bathroom, where all three of us had to shower him. He was too big and heavy for me to hold up and wash at the same time, so my father and Keith held him while I washed him. Throughout this time, he was sleepy and became slightly agitated as he was cold and wanted to go back to bed. He started to shiver with the cold, so I dried and dressed him as quickly as I could. It was like dressing a six-foot, helpless, newborn baby; he couldn't help me at all.

By this time, Christmas dinner had been served in the dining room. It was obvious that Tony would not want to eat so we sat him in a comfortable chair, by a radiator, and tried without too much success to get some fluids into him. He just slept and the rest of the family ate the first and second course of their dinner in what can only be described as a 'strained' Christmas spirit. Our attentions were totally on Tony and what we should do.

I was unable to eat and after everyone had finished the main course I couldn't stand it any longer. I felt that we needed to do something, as Tony didn't seem to be perking up. Everybody agreed that we should call a doctor. My father had not yet registered with a surgery, so we telephoned one of his friends in the village to get the details of the nearest one.

Once I had finished explaining everything to the doctor on the phone, she asked if it was possible to get Tony to the surgery in Tintern, where she had the computer and all of her equipment. She said that she really needed to take a look at him.

My mother came with me for support and also to help carry Tony to and from the car. For the whole time that the doctor was examining Tony and asking us questions, he slept soundly on her couch.

After a short while, the doctor informed us that she thought it best that Tony was taken to the A&E department at the nearest hospital, which was about 25 miles away in Newport. She arranged for an ambulance to collect him from the surgery straight away and my mother and I followed in my car. It was as if I was having a bad dream. It could not be possible; the day before, Tony had been 'normal'.

Chapter Eleven

I began to question what 'normal' was for Tony. When I first met him, he was living on his own in his own house. He kept a very clean, presentable home and was a very good cook. He was a very laid-back, happy soul and a real ladies' man. Everyone who ever met him liked him; there was nothing about him to dislike. He was a loyal friend and a good listener. I have never, ever met an enemy of his and don't believe there are any.

Tony was always easy to be with. I suppose that was due to the fact that he was hardly ever serious and enjoyed life to the full. He made me laugh with his odd sayings and great imitations. We often had parties at home for our friends and family, and Tony was a brilliant host. I would prepare the food and Tony would organise the drink. Tony was a keen wine drinker; he knew a lot about different wines, as his good friend Ian was a wine merchant and taught him about his trade. He also had a passion for Shepherd Neame beer. He would travel miles with Ian, every Wednesday night without fail, to The Woolpack in Brookland on Romney Marsh, as they sold exactly that.

He wasn't a dancer but would move the top half of his body to music while singing along and playing an imaginary guitar or drums and pulling faces that had everyone else in hysterics. He would always manage a smooch with the ladies though, messing around and trying to grab parts of their anatomy: all in the best possible taste, of course.

One of his favourite musicians was Elton John and he had just about every one of his albums. For my birthday one year, Tony surprised me with tickets to see Elton John at Wembley Stadium. It was a hot Sunday in June and over that weekend there was a music festival going on in London. We drove through London, passing various musical events, one being a reggae concert on Clapham Common. The traffic was at a standstill around the common and we sat with the windows open, singing along to UB40, who were another favourite band of Tony's and mine.

We arrived at Wembley just before the start of the concert. The music began at two o'clock with a singer who was unknown to me, and we then heard the wonderful saxophone playing of Curtis Stigers. Eric Clapton played for the rest of the afternoon while we sat with hundreds of other concertgoers on the pitch area of the stadium, enjoying picnics from Fortnum & Mason. The atmosphere was electric and very relaxed on that warm, sunny afternoon. However, the 'piece de resistance' for me had to be when the sun started to go down and Elton John came onto the stage singing 'Don't Let the Sun Go Down on Me'. Tony and I swayed together with our arms around each other, singing at the tops of our voices. I still get goose bumps when I think of that day.

The only negative trait of his that his friends did ever mention, and they mentioned it often, was his stubbornness, but even this they would laugh about in disbelief. They used to say that if there were 12 of them having a discussion, all of them apart from Tony would agree on a certain subject. He would swear black was white and would NEVER give in. I soon learnt what an infuriating trait this was, although I was later to learn that his stubbornness was an asset.

Tony was very much his own man and if there was something he didn't want to do he wouldn't do it, not even for me. This often meant I would attend events without him, whether they were with family or friends. I found this hard to cope with at times because I always felt that, as a couple, we should put ourselves out for each other, even when we didn't particularly want to. I loved him dearly and wanted him by my side at weddings, christenings and parties. His excuse was either that he was too tired or just didn't feel like socialising.

There were many other times when the stubbornness reared its ugly head. Sunday evening for me was ironing night. I would do the washing on Saturday and by Sunday it was dry and ready for ironing. This particular evening, I happened to pass comment on one of the shirts I was ironing. "This shirt that Dad gave you is easy to iron; it's really good quality. Did it feel good to wear?"

"I dunno I didn't wear it!" he replied.

I laughed and said, "Of course you did, I remember you wearing it in the week and as there are only five shirts here for me to iron, you must have done!"

He continued to deny it and was adamant he hadn't worn it. I remember saying something sarcastic along the lines of, "Oh, so I suppose you went topless to work on that day did you?"

At this point, he rose from his chair, unplugged the iron

and launched it across the room in a temper, with me in hot pursuit to retrieve it before it left a scorch mark on the carpet.

No more was said after that, but I remember being in a state of disbelief, not only due to his angry outburst, which really wasn't him, but also because he still denied wearing the shirt. Was this stubbornness or had he really forgotten Dad giving him a shirt and then wearing it?

The long weekdays and endless hours of work with no breaks took their toll on me and I was often signed off work by the doctor with viral-type illnesses. This is why I looked forward to our two, sometimes three, holidays abroad each year. Tony loved the Greek islands and we would often make a last-minute booking on Teletext to go to some relatively unknown and unspoilt island. Although we would do some sightseeing, most of our time was spent at the beach, sunbathing, snorkelling and swimming. In the evenings, we would walk into the back streets of the villages to find the typical Greek restaurants where only the Greek people ate, as this usually indicated a good restaurant and tasty food.

One year we went to Israel for a week of sightseeing in the Holy Land and a week of relaxation in Eilat on the Red Sea. Although Tony wasn't particularly religious, he had a deep fascination with the Holy Land and was interested in the history and the culture.

For our honeymoon, we spent three weeks in the Maldives, where we stayed on an island called Villivaru, which you could walk around in just seven minutes. This was by far the best holiday we had had at that point. It was like paradise on earth. The locals had a saying: 'No news, no shoes'. The island was small and totally sandy with no roads, let alone vehicles, and we spent three blissful weeks wearing no shoes and not having a clue about what was going on in the outside world. On our return, we stopped off for a while at Colombo in Sri Lanka, which was a shock to our system. After staying on an island with only 60 huts, one restaurant and one bar, this place was like Piccadilly Circus!

There were occasions when I got real proof of Tony's love for me, and the 24th April 1993 was one of those days. It was a Saturday morning and I was working overtime with some colleagues at NatWest Stockbrokers, in the offices at Aldgate, on the corner of Mansell Street and Alie Street. I was using the computer when I noticed the lights and the screen flicker. Seconds later, we heard a rumble like thunder, which seemed really strange as the sky was completely blue with not a cloud in sight. Then we felt the shudder: it was as if the windows had turned to cellophane and wavered in the tremor.

Only the previous week, all of the windows in the building had been covered with a bombproof coating as a precaution against a bomb blast. We were extremely grateful for this, as not only were there windows all around the outside of the building but also around the atrium in the middle, stretching from the ground to the fifth floor; therefore, there was a lot of glass to shatter.

Everyone jumped from their seats and ran around the office to see what direction it had come from. It didn't take long to find out. Over in the direction of Liverpool Street station, we saw a huge mushroom cloud rising up into the sky. It rose higher than the NatWest Tower. For a few seconds we all stood in silence and disbelief at what we were witnessing. Then the realisation dawned that some of our colleagues were due into Liverpool Street station at about this time. We started to do a roll call of who travelled into work from that direction and those of us who were already in.

At that moment, it seemed like every phone on our floor started to ring. I picked up my extension to hear Tony's worried voice. He had seen the incident on Sky News and was worried sick. His words to me were, "Are you alright?" When I replied that I was, he answered, "Then get the fuck out of there and get home so that I know you're safe!" That was a rare moment of Tony showing how much he cared for me.

We were told by the police to stay in the building until they advised us that it was safe to leave. We didn't do any work after that; we just watched the police directing cars away from the City. At the Aldgate roundabout the police were stopping cars and buses en route from Whitechapel to the City and filling them with as many passengers as possible to be taken away from the scene. We comforted one of our colleagues who had been on the steps of our building when the blast went off. His feet were knocked from underneath him and he fell to the ground. We were nearly a mile away from where the bomb exploded.

When we were finally allowed to leave the building later in the afternoon, London was like a ghost town. There were no vehicles on the roads and the only sounds to be heard were the alarms ringing out from the office buildings. The powerful effects of the blast had travelled through the maze of streets in the City, hitting some places worse than others. In some areas the office windows on one side of the road were blown out, while on the other they were intact. I felt vulnerable and scared in the almost-benign silence and ran all the way to Tower Hill tube, where I caught a train to Embankment station.

As my train pulled out of Charing Cross, I looked back towards the City and was astonished to see that the blast had even reached as far as the 1 Canada Square building in Canary Wharf. From its windows, printer paper flapped wildly in the wind like party streamers. But this was far from a moment of celebration.

I was immensely relieved to be on my way home to Tony and at that precise moment I never wanted to go back to work in London again, not least on Monday morning. Immediately after walking into the house, I went to Tony and fell into the safety of his arms; I'd never before felt so much comfort from being in his embrace, and I couldn't help thinking of what could have been.

We watched the news together that night and discovered that the IRA had detonated the bomb from a truck parked in Bishopsgate, a major thoroughfare in London's financial district. A news photographer was killed in the explosion and 44 people were injured. I was to learn, years later, that the damage cost £350 million to repair.

Watching the news, the full extent of the bomb blast hit me hard. I suppose it was delayed shock that made me cry with horror, sadness and then relief to have survived, having been so close.

Chapter Twelve

After our first wedding anniversary and over four years of living together, I had started to become quite resentful towards Tony. I was hurt by the way he hardly ever accompanied me to events with friends and family and he didn't help me at all with housekeeping, shopping or DIY. When we were at home I was constantly on the go and he was either watching TV or sleeping on the sofa. It just didn't seem fair to me. I was becoming more and more exhausted with the hours I was working—late nights, early mornings and commuting for four hours daily—and I was depressed with recurrent viral illnesses.

We went through a bad patch like a lot of married couples do, and I was extremely sad at the thought of our relationship failing. Why was it that both my relationships were one-sided? It was me that did everything and seemed to hold everything together, alone. I was tired and wanted to run away from all the pressure, but I couldn't: I just had to get on with it, like I always did. I desperately wanted someone to take care of me for a change. I wanted to receive rather than keep giving.

When Tony started searching for our summer holiday that year, I told him that I couldn't really afford my half of the cost, if the truth were known, he couldn't afford his half either, but he still booked and went away, alone. Although this upset me, I thought maybe the break would do us good. At the same time, my father was going to be in New York on business so he asked if I wanted to join him, all expenses paid. I decided to go, as I needed a break from everything.

I had a fabulous time! I flew out to join my father and was collected, in a white stretch limousine, from Newark Airport by a colleague of his. We drove around the city for a while, taking in the sights before driving out over the Brooklyn Bridge to another colleague's hotel in Morristown, New Jersey, where my father and I stayed for a few days.

On one of the days, we took the train from New York to Washington as my father and his colleagues had a business meeting there. I visited an art gallery, Georgetown University, the White House and lots of shops with the daughter of my father's attorney, who was also called Jim. Later in the week, my father and I flew down to Tampa for a few days by the sea.

As I had booked my trip after my father had booked his flights, I wasn't due to fly home until a day after him. He left and I had another 24 hours to kill before flying back up to New York and then on to London. I lazed around the pool, reading a good book and just soaking up the last few hours of peace and tranquillity.

Over dinner that evening, there was talk of a hurricane on its way, and it was mentioned on the news that flights from Tampa would be severely delayed. I had no choice in the morning but to go to the airport and hope for the best. When booking my internal flight on Continental Airlines back to Newark, I had allowed myself two hours to get from one terminal to the other: plenty of time, or so I thought, to make the check-in for my Virgin flight back to London.

I checked in at Tampa Airport and everything seemed quite calm. It was very windy and rainy but was nothing like hurricane weather, so I felt sure everything would be fine. Just as we were waiting in the lounge to board, a voice came over the loud speaker explaining that our plane had been delayed on its incoming journey and wasn't due to land for another hour. Although I was concerned, I knew I still had time to spare.

We finally took off from Tampa three hours after the scheduled departure time. I started to panic, as this wouldn't give me much time to change terminals for my next flight. The flight turned out to be the most horrifying of all the flights I have ever experienced, and I've lost count of how many that is. It was like something out of a disaster movie. The plane was being thrown around like a ship on rough seas and I sat nervously and rigidly in my seat, my eyes fixed on the forked lightening that illuminated the dark sky outside.

It reminded me of when I was a child, making the journey from my grandparents' house in London to our home in Colchester by road in the fog: a so-called pea-souper fog, because you couldn't see your hand in front of your face. I would be perched rigidly on the edge of the back seat, looking through the gap between my mother's and my father's seats towards the windscreen. I had to do this just in case my father lost the road or didn't see a vehicle ahead and smashed into it; I needed to be his extra pair of eyes. I really don't know what I hoped to achieve in this situation to help the poor pilot out!

People were screaming and being sick and the aircrew had to stay seated for most of the flight. When I did manage to get the attention of one of them, I asked if they would let me leave the plane as soon as the doors were opened so that I could get to the other terminal as quickly as possible. The stewardess agreed and asked me to move down to the front of the plane. Luckily, I only had hand luggage and wouldn't need to hang around waiting for any checked-in luggage.

The plane finally landed to spontaneous applause and cheers of relief, and we arrived at the gate half an hour after my Virgin flight was due to take off for London. During the journey, I had already thought to myself that if the weather was bad all the way down the East Coast then the chances were all flights would be delayed, including my onward one.

As I walked out of the gate, I asked the staff if they would ring through to the Virgin desk to see if my flight had left, and if not tell them that I was on my way. They obliged and to my great relief the flight had not yet left; however, they omitted to tell them that I was on my way. I didn't have time to do much else but run!

I ran as fast as my heavy cabin bag would allow; I felt as if my legs were going to buckle beneath me when I reached the Virgin check-in desk. I was ecstatic to see a member of staff still there and handed them my ticket and passport only to be told I was too late. I asked them to check because I had been told only a few minutes earlier that the plane was still there. After one more check, he returned to tell me that the plane had just left the gate and was taxiing towards the runway. So near, yet so far! If only the crew had mentioned that I was on my way.

I asked if I could get on another flight but was told that I would have to return in the morning as the airport was closing. They also informed me that there was no guarantee I would get onto a Virgin flight the next day. If both my flights had been with the same airline they would have had a responsibility to get me onto the next available flight without further charge; but as this wasn't the case I would probably have to pay for another flight and may not even get one for a few days. I was directed towards a board on the main concourse, which listed details of local hotels. Luckily, the first one I called had rooms available and the receptionist told me where to go to pick up the courtesy bus.

I waited at the bus stop with pilots and plane crew who were going to the same hotel for some shuteye before their next shift. All of a sudden I felt extremely alone and vulnerable. I was 24 years old and had travelled practically all around the world, but this was only the second time I had travelled on my own. I longed so much to be at home safe and sound with Tony, or at least to know that I would be on a flight the next day, but I didn't even have that guarantee.

After queuing for a while at reception I finally got to my room. It was very basic; the toilet didn't flush and the air-conditioning chugged like a train, but it was far too stuffy and hot to switch it off. Unsurprisingly, I didn't get any sleep and was showered, out of the room and on a bus back to the airport by seven the next morning.

I spent the whole of that morning making phone calls and visiting airline desks in a bid to get a flight home. At one point it didn't look promising, but finally one very helpful member of staff managed to get me on a flight that day for just $200. He did have to do a bit of jiggery pokery, which I'm not sure he should have, but I wasn't going to complain, as I just wanted to get home!

Finally, the time came to board the plane. I stored my coat in the overhead locker and settled down, relieved to be going home at last. I was exhausted after my sleepless night and hoped that I would sleep for most of the journey. Just as the crew were about to close the doors for take-off, three officious-looking men in dark suits boarded the plane. They spoke to one of the air stewardesses and then began to walk along the aisle in my direction, while looking up at the seat numbers. When they reached my seat, one of them asked if they could look at my boarding pass. My heart started to pound like a drum in my chest. Was I in trouble? Had that kind man done something illegal? Feeling terrified, I did as he asked and took the boarding pass out of my bag to hand to him.

"When did you purchase your ticket ma'am?" he asked.

"Today," I replied, not wanting to lie and not really feeling the need to.

"Are you able to tell me who sold it to you?" he continued.

I remembered that the young man, who was so obviously flirting with me when he sold me the ticket, had given me his business card in the hope that I would contact him when I returned home. What should I do? If I gave them the card, he would almost certainly get into trouble; why else would these men have bothered to board the plane and speak to me?

At that precise moment, I felt so tired, extremely homesick and very scared. My natural response was therefore to hand the business card over, which I did but not without feeling tremendously guilty over the man who had more than likely risked his job for me!

They obviously got all they needed because they thanked me and exited the plane, enabling us to be on our way. I suddenly became aware that I was holding my breath and let out a massive sigh of relief.

I arrived home late that night when Tony was already asleep in bed. I dropped my bags and crept upstairs to our bedroom. I quietly undressed, slipped into bed next to him and snuggled up to his warm, naked body. I held him tight and never wanted to let him go. I decided at that point that, no matter how difficult our relationship was at times, I never wanted to go on holiday without him again. I knew I never wanted to live without him either!

Chapter Thirteen

So, here I was, four years later, following an ambulance with my darling Tony in it. I hated not being in there with him, holding his hand. The thought of him in there alone tore me to bits, but I guessed that he probably had no clue I wasn't there as he was so sleepy.

During that drive, I started to think back over the previous weeks leading up to Christmas. Had there been any signs that something was wrong? I started to tell my mother about something that happened just the week before Christmas. Tony had had his firm's Christmas party and had inevitably had a lot to drink. When he arrived home that night, he told me all about his evening and we had a laugh.

The next day, while we were at the shops getting some last minute presents, he told me, again, about two of the incidents that he had already told me about the night before. I told him that he was repeating himself, but he really couldn't remember telling me and became quite annoyed, thinking I just wasn't interested in hearing his story; he was adamant that he hadn't already told me. I laughed and said, "Boy you really did have a lot to drink last night didn't you?"

In the nine years that I had known him, it was a very common occurrence for him to really not remember things he had said. I was used to it and always put it down to his stubbornness. I thought that once he had denied it, he couldn't back down even if he did remember. Now I was starting to doubt my reasoning.

By the time my mother and I had arrived at the hospital and parked, Tony had already been taken to a cubicle in the A&E department. We found out where he was and sat by his side to wait for him to be seen by a doctor. He slept the whole time and wasn't even aware that we were there.

As it was Christmas Day, the hospital had a skeleton staff and the other beds were full. We waited hours before Tony was seen but finally when the doctor arrived, Tony woke up. Typical! I felt like a fraud, explaining that Tony had practically not woken up since going to bed on Christmas Eve!

The doctor examined Tony and started to ask him lots of questions, like what his name was, where he lived, his wife's name, and his son's name and age. Tony managed to answer all these correctly, but when the doctor pointed to the watch on his wrist and asked what it was, Tony couldn't answer. He had forgotten the word for it.

The doctor began to ask more questions relating to words that Tony wouldn't use every day, and he discovered from this that he was having a problem with his long-term memory. Words that he used regularly weren't a problem but others were.

After more discussion about what had happened that day, the doctor told us that he would need to keep Tony in hospital overnight under observation. We settled him into a ward and were told as we left to ring in the morning for more news. By this time, Tony was sleeping again and was oblivious to whether we were there or not, which made it easier for me to leave him. My mother and I drove the 25 miles back to the pub in a state of numbness and disbelief, with so many unanswered questions, and no news to reassure the rest of the family with.

Christmas night was a sober affair for us all and I retired to bed relatively early. Thomas was sleeping peacefully in his cot, oblivious to the fact that he wouldn't get his normal cuddles in bed with Daddy in the morning. I wanted to scoop him up and take him to bed with me, but knew that I needed to be with my own thoughts and not have to entertain him if he awoke.

I slept fitfully, but was in a sound sleep when Thomas started chattering away to himself at about eight o'clock the next morning. It was Boxing Day. I got him out of his cot and took him into bed with me, where he immediately asked where Daddy was. How do you explain to a 16 month old that Daddy is in hospital because he can't stay awake and is confused? I really can't remember how I dealt with this one; I just know I did the best I could!

I got up, washed and dressed both Thomas and myself, and went down to join the rest of the family. I tried, without luck, to eat some breakfast before calling the hospital to be told that I could go and collect Tony as soon as I was ready. The nurse was unable to give me any information when I asked a stream of questions, so my mother and I were eager to get on our way to find out more.

When we arrived at the nurse's station they told us that Tony was waiting for us by his bed in the ward. When I asked what they thought the problem had been, they replied that they didn't know and that there wasn't a doctor around to speak to, as it was Boxing Day. That was all they said! I couldn't believe it... I was worried. Tony's behaviour the previous day had been nowhere near normal, so at that point I could only assume that during his night in the hospital he had made a full recovery.

However, when we got to Tony, he wasn't normal at all. He was confused and the sparkle had gone from his eyes. He no longer seemed like the Tony I knew. We got him into the car and began the drive back to the pub. He asked lots of questions about where we were and why he had been in hospital. He also kept asking us, "What's that funny smell?" and each time we couldn't smell a thing. When we asked him what it smelt like, he would say something completely random, like, "It smells like petrol", even though we were nowhere near a petrol station.

After getting back to the pub, we soon realised that Tony was far from well. He seemed really depressed, confused and wasn't able to communicate with us like he used to. He was struggling to find the right words and kept asking what the funny smell was. The thing I noticed more than anything was that something was missing in his eyes; they seemed blank, with no sparkle or life.

We called our own doctor back home and explained what had happened. He was amazed that the hospital had released Tony without giving us an explanation and asked if we could get back to see him that day. We booked the latest appointment with him that we could, packed the car and began the long journey home from Chepstow to Kent. As usual, Thomas was a little angel during the journey, for which I was grateful, as I don't think Tony would have known what to do if he wasn't. My mother followed in her car so that she could be around to take care of Thomas, if needed.

We made it to the doctor's appointment by the skin of our teeth. Our doctor didn't really know Tony as, up until then, he had never had a need to see a doctor; he had always been so fit and healthy. Dr Cooney examined him fully and asked us both lots of questions, after which he was flabbergasted that the hospital had let Tony out. He told us that we needed to go straight to A&E and that he would call through to let them know we were on our way.

After three hours or so spent waiting in a cubicle at the William Harvey Hospital in Ashford, they admitted Tony to a ward, where he stayed for a couple of days. In that time, they did tests, which included a CT scan on his brain. They then told him he could go home and we were to wait for the results.

Nothing had changed in Tony's behaviour and the two weeks we had to wait for results seemed like a lifetime. We spent New Year's Eve at home, both suffering with flu and wondering what the next year had in store for us.

Chapter Fourteen

Finally, the day of Tony's consultant appointment arrived. There had been a heavy dumping of snow during the night so I made sure I got Tony and Thomas ready to leave in good time. I strapped Thomas into his car seat and went back into the house to help Tony to the car; he hadn't been as steady on his feet since the incident on Christmas Day, and the last thing we needed was for him to slip on the ice.

As we entered the main entrance of the hospital, I thought back to the last time I had been in that part of the building; the day we had taken our newborn son home, just 16 months earlier. We'd been full of excitement and joy; Tony had a spring in his step, proudly carrying Thomas in his car seat. I looked round at him on this morning, willing him to be that same young and vibrant man, but all I saw was a sad, sombre face with emotionless eyes looking back at me. He seemed to have aged by 30 years.

Thankfully, we didn't have to wait too long before being called into the consulting room. I'm sure Thomas sensed the seriousness of the occasion, as he sat silent and motionless on my lap as we listened to what was being said.

"It appears the episode that Tony experienced on Christmas Day was an epileptic fit," explained the doctor.

"Thank goodness!" I exclaimed, letting out an enormous sigh of relief. I knew a bit about epilepsy and had heard that with medication people could live a fairly normal life.

The doctor looked at me with concern in his eyes and said, "No, I don't think you understand. The scan has shown up something of concern." He took a scan picture from a brown envelope on his desk, held it up to the light and pointed to a dark grey area in the middle of an otherwise light area. Even without any medical knowledge, I guessed this wasn't normal and assumed that maybe having a seizure had left its mark. But the words that came out of his mouth next hit me in the chest like a thunderbolt.

"It appears that Tony's seizure was caused by pressure on the brain..." at this point he paused before gently delivering the words, "...from a brain tumour."

We sat in silence as the doctor slowly and clearly explained what would happen next, making it easier for us to take it all in. "There is a relatively new procedure out for operating on brain tumours, and, if you both consent, I would like Tony to have the tumour removed in this way." He went on to explain that the new procedure was far less invasive than the old way of operating, and therefore recovery was usually much faster. "If you are happy to go ahead, the surgeon will be able to operate at King's College Hospital in two days' time."

At this point, Tony, who had not yet said a word, sat bolt upright and, with a look of utter terror on his face, cried out, "That soon?"

My heart went out to Tony at the thought of what he must have been going through. Less than a month ago, life was pretty normal and perfect in his eyes; now, here he was facing brain surgery. However, as he explained to me later, he just wanted this 'thing', which was causing him to feel so 'different', out as soon as possible so that he could get back to normal.

I made arrangements for Thomas to stay with my sister and brother-in-law in Colchester while I was with Tony at the hospital. This was the perfect option as he was always very happy to be with them. He had his cousins to play with, so for him it would be nothing but fun and there would be no chance of him missing Tony and me. Equally, I knew, without a doubt, that Thomas would be fine and get all the love and care he needed from my sister. This was a massive weight off my mind and meant I could focus totally on Tony.

The day before Tony was due at the hospital, we drove to Tina and Keith's, where we stayed the night. We left early the next morning for the hospital. We took the train so that I wouldn't have to worry about parking the car for hours on end. Thankfully, the company Tony worked for provided private healthcare for all their staff and this meant that the hospital allowed me to stay in his room with him for the night before the operation. He was so frightened and I really didn't want to leave his side.

The neurosurgeon who was to perform Tony's operation the next day came to explain the details of the procedure and to obtain signatures of consent. He told us that he would drill three very small holes through the skull close to the tumour; one of the incisions would be for a tiny telescopic camera to be inserted, and the others would be for surgical tools. He would insert the tools into the holes at the same time as watching what he was doing on a monitor, which would project images of Tony's brain and the tumour.

He pointed out the risks involved with this type of operation and made us aware of what can go wrong when operating on something as intricate as the brain. The plan was to de-bulk the tumour as much as possible, relieving the pressure on the brain. He explained that Tony had an astrocytoma tumour and that it was in the left temporal lobe, which consists of structures that are vital for declarative or long-term memory. This accounted for his forgetting words that he didn't use on a regular basis.

Finally, he told us that the tumour would be taken away for testing to ascertain what grade of tumour it was and whether or not it was malignant. This was the first time we had heard any mention of the possibility of cancer, and it left us feeling cold.

That night, the wonderfully kind nurses dragged a mattress into the room and made up a comfortable bed for me on the floor, right next to Tony. I was able to lie there, holding Tony's hand as he drifted off to sleep. I didn't sleep well and was already up and washed when the nurse came in to see Tony first thing. Not long after I had eaten some breakfast, my mother arrived at the hospital. She wanted to be with me during the long wait of Tony's operation.

A little while after Tony had his pre-meds, a hospital porter came to take him down for the operation. I was allowed to go as far as the room where they would administer his anaesthetic. He looked so scared and so vulnerable. Fighting back the tears, I kissed him hard on the lips before letting his hand go and walking back through the corridors to where my mother was waiting. All sorts of horrible thoughts were going through my mind as to how he might be when or, worse still, if I saw him again. By the time I reached my mother, I fell into her arms, sobbing uncontrollably. For days, I had held it together for Tony. I wanted to show him that I was confident that everything would be all right, but now all my true worries and doubts came flooding out in my tears.

Tony would be going straight to the High Dependency Unit after his operation, so my mother and I vacated his room and went to the family waiting area, where we waited for just over six hours. During this time, my father arrived from the pub in Wales and we updated him on events so far. This was the first time that I felt upset and annoyed that he was living miles away from home and was not there to support my mother, while she was juggling work and looking after me, Thomas and James. However, my grandparents were nearby and moved into the house to take care of James and the dogs whenever my mother was with me.

Finally, the surgeon, still dressed in his scrubs, walked into the family room. All three of us looked questioningly in his direction and he sat down with us to explain how things had gone. "I am very pleased with how the operation went. I was able to take 90% of the tumour away, without damaging any of the surrounding area. This will be sent away for analysis as previously explained. Tony will be monitored in the High Dependency Unit for the next 24 hours or so before being moved to his own room and I will be visiting him every day until I think he is okay to go home."

"Can we go to see him now?" I asked.

"Yes, of course! He will be a bit groggy but you may see him for a short time." I couldn't get to the High Dependency Unit fast enough and had to stop myself running down the corridors.

My mother came in with me first to see Tony and we couldn't believe how much better he seemed. He was groggy, yes, but he seemed to have some sparkle back in his eyes. After a few minutes, my mother left Tony's bedside allowing my father to visit him with me for a few minutes, and then we both left him to sleep.

My father drove back to Wales and my mother and I got the train back to Tina and Keith's house to give them the news and see my darling little boy! For the first time since hearing about the brain tumour, I allowed an element of hope to enter my mind. Hopefully, they would find that the tumour was benign and Tony would be fine. Yet again, we were playing the waiting game, but it couldn't hurt to be positive... could it?

My mother and I made the journey to the hospital and back from Colchester each day, leaving Thomas with Tina. We spent the time on the train talking non-stop about what might happen. It was all 'ifs' and 'buts', but it was good therapy for us both. I was so grateful to have my dear mother there to talk to in those hours spent on the train and waiting; I'm sure she kept me sane! It must have been the hardest thing for her, worrying about what would become of her son-in-law, who she adored, but also feeling concern for her daughter and grandson.

Each day we saw more and more improvement in Tony, and after four days he was allowed home. Dick, one of the

Directors at Tony's office, had been in continual contact with me since we first told him of the situation, always asking if we needed anything. He arranged for a car to collect us from the hospital and take us back to Tina's in Colchester, to collect Thomas and our car.

As we walked into Tina's house, Thomas came running up to Tony, squealing with excitement and putting his arms out to be picked up. Tony scooped him up and gave him the biggest squeeze cuddle ever!

Chapter Fifteen

During the weeks that followed, Tony seemed to improve. His eyes showed more expression; we saw his wonderfully infectious smile again, and some of his old fun character started creeping back. He was much less confused, although, from time to time, he was forgetful.

For as long as I had known Tony, he had smoked small Hamlet cigars, but only ever three or four a day. He wouldn't smoke a whole one all at once; he would have some, leave it in the ashtray and then light it up again later in the day. For some reason, after the seizure on Christmas Day, he just stopped smoking completely. He never mentioned it and obviously I didn't feel the need to offer his cigars to him. However, a couple of weeks after his operation, as he sat in his armchair, he asked, "Did I used to smoke?"

"Yes," I replied. "You used to smoke Hamlet cigars but haven't had one since Christmas Eve."

"Why's that?" he replied.

"I don't know sweetheart. Weird isn't it? Why? Do you fancy one now?" I asked.

"I don't know, do I?"

"How would I know?" I responded, laughing.

After a pause, he went on, "Do you think I got this because

of smoking?"

I assumed he was referring to the tumour, and replied, "No, I doubt it. Why don't you have one if you want one?"

"No, I don't think I want one actually," he replied, with a shrug. We had that very same conversation on a few more occasions, and eventually he did start smoking again.

Prior to going into hospital for his operation, Tony had been prescribed steroids to help bring the inflammation down in his brain. The doctor monitored the amount that he took regularly because they only wanted to give him what he needed and no more. You see, there were side effects to taking this medication, one being muscle weakness.

Tony's muscles started to become quite weak, so our doctor arranged for an occupational therapist to visit to see how we could make his life, and also my life, easier. He was too heavy for me to be lifting him out of chairs, so we were given a seating pad, which raised Tony's armchair seat. This meant that he didn't have to push himself up so far each time he got out of the chair.

Not being a driver, Tony had been used to walking here, there and everywhere, and he actually missed being able to do so. He hated being cooped up indoors and missed being able to get some fresh air each day. When we did go anywhere, it had to be in the car, as he wouldn't manage being on his legs for long.

So, the ultimate godsend we received was a wheelchair! It meant that all three of us could get out every day for some fresh air. We would often load the wheelchair into the boot of the car and go further afield. One of our favourite walks at the time was along the Royal Military Canal at Hythe in Kent. As

I wasn't able to push both a wheelchair and a buggy, Thomas would sit on Tony's lap and they would watch the wildlife together, seeing who could spot the biggest fish on the surface of the water.

However relieved I was to be able to get out as a family, it broke my heart to see our toddler sitting on the knee of his daddy in a wheelchair. What I wanted was my fit, ex-footballer and referee husband back and pushing his son in a buggy. For now, though, I had to be grateful for what we had.

There were other side effects to the steroids, which meant that Tony ended up taking a cocktail of medication, all counteracting the side effects of the others. One of the tablets made him physically sick and the only way this could be prevented was by giving him anti-sickness suppositories, which were to be administered by me.

It was the most humiliating experience for Tony, as he lay on his side while the nurse showed me how to insert the suppository into his rectum. Understandably, he was tense and this made the whole procedure very difficult for us both. After about a week of practice, though, I managed to turn it into quite a slick operation and Tony thought nothing of it.

As it was, this turned out to be the first of many upsetting and degrading times for Tony, but he was always the most considerate and easy-to-care-for patient. He never stopped apologising for being an inconvenience, and that made these moments all the more heart-wrenching for me.

The days and weeks leading up to our next appointment, when we would get the results of the biopsy, seemed endless and the wait went on longer than we were told to expect. It got to a point where I was ringing the hospital at least once every day to find out what was happening. Each phone call left me more and more stressed because they could never tell me anything or, if they did, it was just that they hadn't managed to get all the consultants together at one time to discuss the results.

I wasn't sleeping well because each night, as I got into bed, the 'what ifs' just wouldn't stop churning over in my brain. That bloody 'C' word just would not leave my head! I had always been a fairly positive person, but at night when everyone was sleeping I struggled to remain so. What if the results showed cancer? What then?

I was so grateful to have my mother and my friend and neighbour, Lorraine, nearby to take my mind off the negativity during my waking hours. Those two wonderful ladies kept me sane throughout, and gave me the strength to stay strong for my dear husband and darling son.

Finally! After about three of the longest weeks in my life, we received a date for the appointment the following week. I felt an enormous sense of relief and anxiety in equal measure. Whatever the news was, surely it would be better to know than to go through the utter agony of not knowing and always surmising. At least we would have a grasp on what we were dealing with and could focus on getting Tony better.

Rather than having to traipse up to Kings College Hospital in London again, we were able to see the neurosurgeon that operated on Tony at the Chaucer Hospital, a private hospital in Canterbury, which was about half an hour's drive from our home. My mother came to our house to be with Thomas so that we didn't have to take him with us. Tony and I hardly spoke on the journey to the hospital. My brain was just too exhausted from all the 'thinking' that I'd been doing in previous weeks and Tony's brain... well, who knows what thoughts the poor darling had going on in there. It didn't bear thinking about!

I was enormously pleased to see the surgeon again; I felt like he was the one person who was qualified to, and could, answer every question I had. I had spent the last two months scouring the one medical book I had at home, looking for answers but obviously not finding any firm ones. Every brain tumour sufferer's situation is different, and all I had been doing was driving myself mad with desperation, and to no avail.

The surgeon delivered his findings, as he always did, in a slow, gentle and caring way. "I'm afraid, Tony, your tumour was found to be malignant."

I gasped and felt tightness in my chest as an almost silent, uncontrollable sob escaped from my mouth. No! They must have it wrong! Tony was too young! I realised immediately how ridiculous this thought was, as thousands of young people and children die from cancer every year; I just never thought it would happen in our family.

"The good news..." the surgeon continued.

"There's good news?" I thought, unbelieving.

"... is that we think the tumour is only a grade 2 astrocytoma and people with this type of tumour have been known to live 10 years or more."

Ten years! Was that all? The first thing that went through my mind was that Thomas would only be 11 years old. He couldn't lose his daddy at that age! Tony would be 51, which was no age to die, and I would only be 39. That's no age to become a widow, either!

The surgeon then went on to explain that they would like to give Tony a course of radiotherapy. They needed to destroy any other cancer cells that may be present in the remaining 10% of the tumour, which wasn't operable due to the risk of damaging his brain. Tony was to have the treatment in the Oncology Department of the Kent & Canterbury Hospital, and the course would be every weekday for six weeks. However, the treatment would not start for a few weeks, as they needed to let the inflammation in the brain (caused by the operation) reduce.

He gave us all the facts and a huge amount of anecdotal evidence; however, we also had many questions that he couldn't answer, as no doctor, consultant or medical professional can ever know what will really happen when a person has cancer.

I had told the doctors previously that, when I first met Tony, I noticed that the pupil in his right eye never dilated; as he and his mother had not noticed this in the previous 30 odd years, they deduced that it probably hadn't been like it since birth. It was because of this that they thought the tumour had been around for some years and almost certainly for the whole time that I had been with Tony.

I wondered, then, if this explained a lot of Tony's unusual behaviour during our time together, particularly his stubbornness. Was he being stubborn or did he really believe what he remembered or was saying? Was this why he did nothing at weekends, with the working week and long commute taking all his energy and meaning he had to recover? I have to admit that this news filled me with guilt; how many times had I got angry and frustrated at his behaviour and his laziness, when really he couldn't help it?

The surgeon's final words to us that day, as we left, were, "Now go away and get on with living the rest of your life!" What? With this hanging over our heads! How on earth do we do that?

However, I thought to myself as we left the hospital: the brain is an amazing organ. Not only can it heal itself, but you can also train it to keep you thinking positively and believing that things can improve and even change for the better. Maybe, just maybe, they were wrong and Tony would go on to live well into his 80s! That was what we had to believe!

Chapter Sixteen

During the following weeks, we made huge attempts to live as normal a life as possible. I was constantly on the phone speaking to friends and family who would call to see how he was doing, and although in one way this was much-needed therapy for me, in other ways it was exhausting.

When I wasn't on the phone, I was playing with Thomas, caring for Tony, cooking or doing the housework, usually while listening to music. Listening to music has always been so important to me; I enjoy it more than watching TV. It can bring back happy and sad memories in an instant and has often been my solace.

One artist I would listen to was Celine Dion, and many of the lyrics of her songs resonated with me at that time. I would sing along at the top of my voice, feeling all sorts of strong emotions. Sometimes, especially when listening to 'Call the Man', it was all too much and I couldn't sing for sobbing. But that was fine; if it made me release my sadness that was a good thing, right?

We regularly had friends and family pop by to spend time with Tony, which he absolutely loved. At the time, it really pepped him up. However, he would pay for it the following day and would sleep longer.

I don't think he had realised prior to this just how highly thought of he was. He always seemed amazed that people bothered to travel miles just to see him! Regularly, Directors and colleagues from his work would take the train from London to spend a few hours with him. The Directors even allowed those staff that worked closely with Tony to have the day off to visit him without using up their holiday allowance. He enjoyed hearing all the office gossip and catching up with events.

The company he worked for offered us never-ending support throughout the time he was unable to work. They paid him in full every month and even gave him his profit share and bonus, regardless of the fact that he hadn't worked in the qualifying period. For this I was immensely grateful; even if I had been working when Tony became ill, I wouldn't have been able to then as Tony needed 24-hour care. Life goes on and the mortgage and bills have to be paid, even when your husband has cancer! This was one area of our life that I didn't need to worry about.

Dick, the Director who sent a car to collect us from the hospital after Tony's operation, even called me one day to say that the company would be willing to fly Tony out to the States to have a new, pioneering treatment that they would cover the cost of. That's how highly thought of he was. Tony, however, said he couldn't and wouldn't allow them to do this for him.

Thomas continued to be a happy, funny and endearing child, and brightened our every day. It was very hard to feel sad when we had him around and we regularly spent hours each day laughing at his antics.

I was always very aware that the only time Tony's eyes lit up was when he looked at Thomas. Whereas, when he looked at me that was a different matter. Most of the time, his eyes were emotionless but there were times when I thought I almost saw hate in them and it cut like a sword through my heart. This man that I adored and was so scared of living my life without seemed to dislike everything about me and I didn't understand why.

However, Tony still managed at times to show me that he cared. We took a trip to Hastings one day to have a walk by the sea. We ate lunch in a swish Italian restaurant, after which I pushed Tony and Thomas, in the wheelchair, to the shops as Tony said he wanted to treat me to something to thank me for everything I was doing for him. I told him it wasn't necessary, that I did it out of love for him and, quite apart from anything else, he was an easy patient to take care of.

He still insisted and ended up buying me a silk, lime-green scarf, which made me feel bright and cheerful when I put it on. It was the first time in a long time that he had had to sign a credit card slip, and I noticed how he struggled to sign his name. His signature was shaky and nothing like it was normally. It made me very aware that I might need to have him add me to his bank account as a second signatory.

Tony and I had always had separate bank accounts, and since I had stopped work when Thomas was born Tony had paid all the household bills, transferring housekeeping money to my account so that I could do the food shopping. I was concerned that if ever he were not in a fit state to transfer money to me, or to sign cheques for unexpected bills, we could end up in trouble and I might not be able to feed us. I made a note to myself to bring the subject up at another time. We had had a lovely day; he had made a kind gesture by buying me a scarf and now wasn't the time. I knew it would be a difficult conversation to have, as Tony could feel that his role as head of the household was being taken away. It would also remind him of the fact that he was losing some of his faculties.

After a few weeks, we finally felt as if things were moving along with his planned treatment because Tony had to go to the hospital to have a facemask made. They applied a substance to his face, neck and part of his head, avoiding the eye, nose and mouth areas, and allowed it to set before removing it and drilling screw holes into the flaps they had left on each side of the mask. Using technology and x-ray, they marked a spot on the mask, indicating the exact point that they had to zap with radiotherapy each time Tony had a treatment. The mask would enable them to fix Tony to the bed in the exact spot that he needed to be for his treatments, without fear of him being able to move. It was vitally important that they only zapped the cancerous cells and didn't damage any of the good cells.

For the first couple of weeks, Tony coped very well with the treatment. He'd been used to having an afternoon nap, but during this time he would go straight to bed as soon as we returned home from the hospital and sleep for a bit longer. The visits didn't turn out to be as unbearable as we expected, due, I think, to Thomas setting the tone on the first day. The waiting area was a long corridor with the treatment rooms leading off from it. There was seating along the wall on one side, where people sat in silence, waiting for their name to be called. I noticed that everyone there seemed to be in their 70s and older, and they all looked sympathetically at Tony and then Thomas. Thomas was calling us 'Mummy' and 'Daddy', so it didn't take much for them to realise that one of the parents of this toddler had cancer.

The seating area faced the opposite wall of the corridor, which had a mural of a country scene all the way along it. There were green fields, trees, flowers, rabbits, ducks, birds and a horse looking right at us from over a five-bar gate. Well, Thomas was in his element! He spotted the horse and while standing in the corridor, between the waiting patients and the horse, he immediately started singing, all the time pointing his finger in the air and moving it to the beat. "Horsey, horsey don't you stop, just let your feet go clippedy-clop. Let your tail go swish and your wheels go round. Giddy up! We're homeward bound!"

When he'd finished the whole waiting room erupted in laughter and cheers, clapping their hands enthusiastically. I think Thomas really warmed the cockles of their hearts and made their visits each day much more pleasurable. Whenever we arrived each day, they would all call out in chorus, "Hello Thomas! Are you going to sing for us today?" And of course he did, every time, and not just once! He really played to the crowd and this usually sombre waiting room became a hive of excitement whenever we were there, for which we, the other patients and the staff were grateful!

Chapter Seventeen

By three weeks into his daily treatments, Tony was sleeping for longer and longer each day; so much so that he was hardly out of bed. We knew to expect this but there were other signs that started to concern me. He seemed to be experiencing more pain in his head and he was struggling to see clearly; this obviously made him depressed.

My sister's brother-in-law, Darren, who I went to school with, and his wife Tresa, came to visit for the weekend and we decided to have a family day out to the Rare Breeds Centre in Woodchurch, not far from home. We thought the fresh air would be good for Tony and seeing Thomas and Darren and Tresa's little boy, Luke, playing with the animals might pep him up a bit.

However, it turned out to be the absolute worst thing for Tony. As we were pushing him around the farm in his wheelchair, he complained of severe pains in his head and said that he couldn't see. This worried us all and I decided that he needed to see a doctor, so we got back to the car as quickly as possible to head for home.

While we were strapping the children into their car seats, Tony was violently sick in the car park. I assumed this was due to the pain he was experiencing. Before having Thomas, I suffered from migraines, which would make me physically sick if I wasn't able to get home from work in time, so I understood how he must have been feeling.

By the time we arrived home, Tony could hardly stand and was almost unconscious, so I immediately called for an ambulance. I went in the ambulance with him and Darren and Tresa stayed at the house to take care of Thomas. This was another one of the many times I was grateful to have my friends around! On arrival at the hospital, Tony was seen by a doctor almost immediately and taken straight to a ward to be monitored overnight. I was told to call in the morning for news.

The following day was like a whirlwind. On the orders of the neurosurgeon who had operated on Tony, our local hospital had him transported by ambulance to King's College Hospital first thing in the morning. I threw some clothes and wash items into a bag and my mother made her way to our house. At 8am, we left home for the two-hour drive to my sister's house with Thomas. Just as we pulled into their drive, the phone was ringing. It was the neurosurgeon asking where I was. I froze, wondering why he was asking and thinking that something awful had happened. He said that he needed to operate on Tony urgently but needed me to sign the papers.

Tears welled up in my eyes, as I felt hugely guilty for not being at my husband's bedside and for delaying the treatment, which could quite possibly be lifesaving. If he died, it would be my fault! I felt like I was being reprimanded by the headmaster for being late and I lamely explained that I had had to take Thomas to be cared for by my sister before I could get to the hospital. I informed him that we were leaving straight away for the station to get a train to London.

I needed to be in two places at once and I couldn't be! Thank heavens again for my darling sister, who immediately began to make Thomas giggle and occupy him with plans of what he and Auntie Tina were going to get up to that day. I was at least able to go straight back out the door again without a worry for how Thomas was; Auntie Tina and TretheweyPewey, as she fondly nicknamed her nephew, would be absolutely fine!

When my mother and I arrived at the hospital, we were taken immediately to the neurosurgeon's office, where we found him already in his scrubs ready to operate on Tony. Even though he had had to wait hours for us to arrive, knowing that every minute counted, his bedside manner was as always the best I have ever known from a medical professional.

He calmly and gently explained that the cause of Tony's downhill spiral could be one of two things: either he had meningitis (inflammation of the brain), which could be cured with antibiotics, or worse, the tumour had grown back. The only way he could confirm either way was by operating.

"The thing is..." he continued, "...and the reason that I need you to sign a document, Alison, is because there are some big risks to Tony undergoing brain surgery again so soon. The brain is a very delicate organ and Tony could possibly come out of the operation in a much worse state than he was before. He could be left permanently brain-damaged and in need of much more care than he currently needs."

He also indicated that there was a risk of even worse than

that! However, I don't know if it was the way he explained it, but he made the decision a very easy one for me and I signed on the dotted line.

I was then 'advised' to go and see Tony before they took him down for his operation. Before walking to his side, I took a few deep breaths to prevent the tears from flowing. For some reason, at that moment, I felt like I could possibly be saying 'goodbye' to my darling man and I didn't want to. There wasn't much time so I held his hand, kissed him long and hard on his cheek, and told him I loved him, before walking away out of his sight and breaking down into floods of tears.

"Oh Mum, that was awful! I might never see him again, or if I do, not in the way he should be." My mother held me tightly but was unable to find any words through her own tears.

Just under six hours later, we were back in the surgeon's office. "I'm afraid my worst fears have been confirmed," he explained. "The tumour has grown back in the few short weeks since Tony's first operation." He took his time delivering the news, almost checking how we were after each sentence. My mother and I sat in stunned silence and I found myself searching his face for any inkling of hope, but to no avail.

He continued: "The tumour has grown back into the cavity left by the removal of the tumour previously, which means that it's a grade 4, the fastest-growing type, not a grade 2 as I first thought."

Then, devastatingly, he added, "If it were my wife, I wouldn't put her through anymore radiotherapy treatment. It should now be a case of having a good quality of whatever life he has left and not having to endure the agony of the treatment."

Finally, from the depths of my dry mouth, I found my voice and asked croakily: "So how long do you think he has?"

"That's always hard to say but with this type of aggressive tumour I would be surprised if he saw a year."

Chapter Eighteen

Tony recovered well from the operation, with no sign of permanent brain damage. In fact, because the pressure on his brain had been eased again he seemed considerably better and even appeared to have a bit of his old personality back.

The thing is, up until the point of us seeing the first signs of Tony ever having a brain tumour, he was a healthy 41 year old. He had always looked after his body, getting regular exercise and fresh air and eating healthily. He was young and, apart from what was going on in his brain, he was fit. He also had so much to live for and couldn't bear the thought of not seeing his son grow up. This made it impossible for him to give up on life, so he decided to carry on with the radiotherapy treatment. It was a relief for me to see him with this attitude and we both had the thought that if we believed enough then maybe, just maybe, he could prove the medical professionals wrong.

Apart from extreme tiredness, he succeeded on seeing the treatment through to the end without further problems and his final session fell on his birthday, 19th May. On this day, his mother took him to the hospital, as I'd arranged a surprise party for his return at lunchtime and needed to be at home to prepare. I had invited about 20 of his close friends, family and work colleagues, and they were all there to surprise him on his return home. Yet again, he was overwhelmed that people had gone out of their way to come and see him and he enjoyed spending the afternoon catching up with them all.

His hair had started to fall out in clumps a couple of weeks previously and he thought he looked stupid with bald patches here and there, so I shaved it all off. He was very proud of his smoothly shaved head and kept removing his Arsenal cap to get everybody to 'have a feel'.

Thomas excitedly helped his daddy by blowing out the candles on his cake and unwrapping the many gifts he received. All in all, his birthday celebrations were a real success and served to pep him up no end.

Dr Cooney would visit him at home regularly, usually having to go up to our bedroom, where Tony was sleeping, to run through a series of physical checks. One of the tests was to check for reflexes by running his pencil up the sole of Tony's foot. Now, Tony couldn't bear touching his own feet as they were so sensitive, let alone anyone else; he wouldn't even allow me to dry them after I had helped him bathe. The first time the doctor did it, Tony snapped, "You ever do that again and I'll 'ave you!" The thought of Tony having the energy at that time to jump out of bed and ''ave' him amused us all, but Tony was deadly serious.

One time, Dr Cooney walked into the room and entered into conversation with Tony as usual. "How you doing Tone!" he asked.

"Still alive, so I must be okay," Tony replied positively.

"You managed to go fishing yet?" The doctor was referring to a conversation that they'd had previously about Tony being determined to sit on a riverbank again.

"No, but... ah you bastard! I told you!" Dr Cooney, who had been pacing up and down at the end of the bed with his pencil surreptitiously at the ready, grabbed the chance to run it up the sole of Tony's foot, catching him unawares. We all burst into eruptions of laughter, and even Tony joined in after he'd recovered from the shock!

Tony continued to do really well in the months to follow. The treatment obviously made some difference, as the GP was able to significantly reduce the amount of steroids he was taking, which helped him to regain some of his strength. He no longer needed to use his wheelchair when we went out.

Thankfully, Tony did become well enough to go fishing again. One sunny day in the summer, I packed up a picnic, loaded Thomas, Tony and all his fishing gear into the car and drove over to fetch Tony's mum, Hazel. Tony chose a pretty section of the River Rother in the village of Kenardington, not far from Hazel and Terry's home in Appledore, and although on this occasion the fish successfully managed to avoid Tony's net, we did have a really pleasant afternoon.

We sat in the warm sun eating our picnic and feeling very content to see Tony back doing normal things again. Thomas was fascinated by the dragonflies dive bombing the water and the water bugs skating on the surface. He, like Tony, loved nothing more than being outdoors and was so exhausted from running up and down the riverbank that he very quickly fell asleep in his car seat on the way home.

A couple of days later, my mother was paying us one of her regular visits when Tony announced that he was going out for a bike ride... alone! My mother and I both looked at him, ready to tell him that we didn't think it was a good idea; it was so hard to accept that he was fit enough, and safe enough, to take to the main roads on his pushbike after being so weak and poorly only weeks earlier. However, there was just no stopping him; his old stubborn streak reared its head and he was going whether we liked it or not!

All we could do was reluctantly wave him off, telling him to stick to the route we had given him so that we would know where to go looking for him in the event that he didn't return. He did return, tired but exhilarated, and it was a wonderful sight to behold; not only seeing his joy at being 'allowed out alone', but being able to breathe again knowing that he was safe.

We enjoyed a lovely, hot summer, passing our days with visits to friends, trips out or just relaxing in the garden. Each morning, Tony would get up, immediately open the patio doors to let the sunshine in and proceed to spend every hour that he wasn't sleeping in the garden watching Thomas play. The sunshine definitely helped to lift our moods.

One particular morning, 31st August, Tony followed his normal routine while I was up in the bathroom, when out of the blue I heard him yell, "Oh my god, Alison, come quick!" I bolted out of the bathroom at double-quick speed, wondering what had happened; I seemed to have spent my days on tenterhooks ever since Tony had first become ill, waiting for the next seizure.

However, on this occasion he was fine, just rooted to the spot in front of the TV. As I looked at the screen, I heard the words "Diana has been killed in a car accident". My first reaction was "Diana who?" Then the penny dropped... Diana, the Princess of Wales, was dead!

For the following few days, Tony and I hardly moved away from the TV. I took the news very badly, like most people all around the world. I needed to grieve for this beautiful and amazing lady.

Thankfully, for Tony though life still went on and seeing the amazing improvement in him since his last operation led me to believe, rightly or wrongly, that the surgeon had got his prognosis wrong and that Tony was going to survive all of this. I started to allow myself to have high hopes for the future and I'm quite sure Tony felt the same.

Chapter Nineteen

All things considered, we had a good summer. It was a bittersweet time; Tony was at home because he was still unfit for work, but this also meant that Thomas and I got to spend some very treasured moments with him, time that most fathers don't get to spend with their young children as they are working all hours. We made the most of our days with Tony's improved health.

However, by the end of September the tide turned and Tony's health started to deteriorate again. All the previous symptoms returned. He had extreme tiredness and headaches, which just kept getting worse to the point that he needed more steroids, more and more pain relief, and a whole other cocktail of drugs. Again, he lost muscle tone and strength and needed his wheelchair when we went out.

It wasn't long before I came to the realisation that this was it; the beginning of the end. There was nothing anyone could do to save my darling man now. This was exactly what the consultant had told us would happen; he was right after all.

I would often sit between Tony's legs, on the floor facing him, as he sat in his chair, holding his hands and chatting. I wanted to savour every last moment I had with him. One day, during one of these times, I wasn't able to hold back my tears as I asked him, "How will I ever live without you?"

He smiled, squeezed my hand and said, "You'll be okay, you've got my bestest boy to take care of you." He was of course referring to Thomas, who had only just turned two years old.

Our vicar, Mike, who had married Tony and me only six years previously, had become a very good friend during the previous months. He visited regularly and provided great comfort to Tony, lessening his fear of dying by comparing it to waiting for a bus that was to take him on the next leg of his journey. He would sit on the floor with Thomas to play with his Duplo bricks. One day, Thomas got confused and called Mike by the name of my father's dog, Tchaik. From that day on, Thomas always called him Tchaik!

Mike was always there for me too, emotionally as well as practically. He repaired the latch on our back gate and not only did he suggest moving our bed down into the dining room, he even helped my mother and me to carry out the removals; moving the bed down and the dining room table and chairs up.

As the weeks passed by, Tony's health deteriorated at a rapid rate and it had become increasingly difficult for me to keep a watchful eye on him when he spent most of the day upstairs in bed. Moving the bed downstairs meant that I could look after both him and Thomas and get on with household chores. Thomas was free to get up on the bed with his daddy for cuddles whenever he wanted, and Tony was able to watch his little boy play, which was the highlight of his every waking hour.

Each night, it would take me ages to fall asleep with the constant thought of life without Tony and the worry that I wouldn't be awake to hold him when he took his final breath. Even when I did drift off, I was still alert to the sounds of his breathing and snoring and would wake immediately with any change. The stress and very little sleep began to take their toll on me and my mother moved in to help me care for Thomas and Tony. My grandparents moved into my parents' house to take care of the dogs and James.

It was at this time that Tony was given diamorphine, as his pain was becoming more severe and his normal painkillers weren't touching it. This made him become very confused and he would often have hallucinations, thinking that he could see insects crawling all over the floor. When I told him that there was nothing there he would get angry and insist that there was, so I would pretend to scoop them all up and put them out in the garden, which seemed to settle him until the next time.

During these weeks, my poor mother was driving back and forth to Canterbury to work, but she still managed to support me in every possible way, including potty training Thomas! It had been the last thing on my mind and she saved me from this well-known challenging time in a child's upbringing; she just got on with it and I hardly noticed the transition from nappies to potty. My mother was giving me the gift of being totally with Tony in his final days as well as still having my funny and joyful son around to help brighten each day. She was also the person that I could open my heart to and who gave me the much-needed hugs that I could no longer have from my husband.

We were provided with a commode, as Tony was unable to get upstairs to the bathroom. He understandably hated using this, as he had very little privacy in our large through lounge/diner, and always tried to get me to take him upstairs. I had to explain that if he fell on the stairs I wouldn't be able to save him and eventually he would give in; however, we had the same argument every time he needed the toilet. For someone who at this time was so frail and weak, he could sometimes show amazing strength and determination. One day, as my mother and I took him to the commode, he resisted strongly, locking his knees so that we couldn't sit him down. He pushed us both aside, stumbled out to the kitchen and started to relieve himself in the sink; pee was bouncing off the dirty plates in the bowl and spraying all over the place. My mother and I just stood in amazement and laughed.

Then there was the night that we were just about to go to bed and he indicated that he wanted to go upstairs to the bathroom. He was hardly able to speak anymore at this point and was practically blind, but he made it very clear that that was what he wanted and he wouldn't give in, becoming quite stressed when we kept refusing. We were concerned as he was so weak and wasn't able to take many steps. He would be a dead weight if he were to fall on us, and we would all come tumbling down the stairs.

However, my mother and I decided to go along with it, as we knew he would try to do it anyway, with or without our help. It was a long, slow process getting him to the bathroom but we made it. Goodness knows where he found the strength and energy, having eaten nothing for the previous seven weeks; it was all I could do to get a sip of water down him and he absolutely refused the food replacement drinks that he was prescribed.

I sat on the side of the bath waiting for him to finish, and as I went to get some toilet paper for him, he snapped: "Only three squares, no more!" This was the first time I'd heard this, and it was yet another of his little quirky traits that I had got to see by being involved in every little private moment of his life. It made me chuckle.

All three of us managed the mammoth task of getting back downstairs safely, and as I tucked Tony up in bed I thought again about how stubborn he could be. However, this time, unlike in years gone by, I was grateful for the stubbornness that his friends had warned me about years ago, as it had given us more precious time with him.

Chapter Twenty

It was as if Tony knew what the next day would bring when he requested the trip to the bathroom that night. The following morning, I awoke at about eight o'clock and the very first thing I became aware of was an intense heat emanating from his body; he was burning up. I moved closer to cuddle up to him and noticed that he had his eyes open in a fixed gaze and didn't react at all to me touching him. It seemed like he was in a semi-conscious state and somehow my instinct told me that this was it; this was the day that I'd been holding my breath for.

I stayed lying next to him, holding his warm but very frail body and never wanting to let him go. I spoke to him, hoping that he could still hear me. "Do you remember our wedding day? I was so, so happy and proud to become your wife. I will always be grateful for the years I have spent with you and for the son you have given me. You have made me the happiest woman alive and you will continue to live on in my heart forever."

I don't remember everything I said. Every thought that came into my head about our time together came out, and throughout all my words and tears Tony didn't respond to me at all, but I just knew he was listening. I gave him a long, lingering kiss on his lips and then left his side to go and find my mother, who was upstairs.

Thankfully, Thomas was still asleep and didn't see my outpouring of emotion as I explained to my mother. She came downstairs with me to see Tony, and like me, she spoke to him, comforting him and stroking his forehead. I left her with him while I went for a quick wash; I didn't want to leave his side for any longer than I had to.

While I was in the bathroom, I heard Thomas cheerfully chatting and singing to his toys, the way he did every morning when he woke up. I lifted him from his cot, barely able to speak as I fought back my tears. I kissed him and hugged him tightly. He leaned back in my arms and stared questioningly at my face, knowing there was something wrong, as I wasn't my normal chatty self, but totally oblivious to just how both our lives were about to change forever.

"Daddy's still fast asleep, Thomas." I told him as I put him down on the chair in the lounge. "So don't go jumping on the bed yet." I didn't want him to see that Tony wasn't reacting, for fear of it frightening him.

Once I had given him his breakfast and washed and dressed him, I carried him over to where Tony lay, motionless, and gently placed him alongside him. "Daddy's still very sleepy but you can give him a big kiss and a cuddle, and then how about if I take you over to Lorraine's to play with Laura for a while?"

Full of excitement at the thought of going to play with his friend, he almost jumped off the bed straight away, forgetting about kisses and cuddles. "No, come on Thomas," I said. "Give Daddy a nice cuddle and a big kiss." I couldn't bear to think of their last moments together being of Thomas wanting to be somewhere else.

Biting my lip as hard as I could to stop the tears, I rushed across the road in my slippers, with Thomas in my arms, to Lorraine's house. I rang the doorbell but there was no reply, so I went to the back door. Lorraine came to the door, soaking wet and wrapped in a towel, having been in the shower. Taking one look at me, she stretched out her arms to take Thomas from me. "Come 'ere darlin', do you want to play with Laura? She's in the front room." With that, Thomas struggled out of her arms and ran off to find Laura.

I couldn't speak; I just sobbed and tried unsuccessfully to tell Lorraine what was happening. She knew and just hugged me close for a few seconds before letting me go back to Tony. "Thomas'll be fine here, don't worry. Give Tony a big kiss for me."

That day turned out to be the longest and saddest day of my life. My darling Tony fought so hard to stay with us. Apart from when I made visits to the bathroom, I lay by his side, holding him all day; his mother was on his other side.

My sister and brother-in-law came to say their goodbyes. My mother kept us all fed and watered, and my father made regular visits over the road to check on Thomas. Although I know he wanted to be there for me, he didn't cope well with watching Tony fight on and listening to his rattling breath. On a couple of occasions, he asked why somebody couldn't do something to ease his passage. "They wouldn't let a dog go through this!" he said, feeling very distraught. I was, however, grateful that he kept visiting Thomas, as I just didn't want to leave Tony's side.

Terry sat quietly for the most part, watching us from a

distance. Goodness knows what must have been going through his mind at the thought of losing his only son and seeing his wife's despair. The only time Tony reacted in any way that day was when Mike was saying some final prayers; he let out a groan, almost as if he was saying 'Amen'.

At half past six that evening, Tony took his final breath. I howled like a large animal in pain, so loud that our neighbours knew exactly when he had gone. My whole body physically ached with the pain of losing him. After a while, I lay by his side, silent and still, all the energy having left my body. When the nurse and doctor came over to do whatever it was they had to do, they almost had to prise me from him; I just didn't want to let him go for the last time.

I don't remember too much about the next hour or so. Mike and the nurse just took over and did what was necessary. Eventually, Mike gently told us to say our final farewells and suggested that we all go upstairs before the undertakers arrived. When we all returned downstairs, all was quiet and our bed was empty; my darling husband had left our home for the last time.

I felt numb and too exhausted to even cry anymore, so I felt it was a good time to fetch Thomas. My father had taken his pyjamas over earlier in the day and Lorraine had given him a bath and dinner; by the time I got there he was sound asleep on the sofa. I spoke to Lorraine and Dennis for a while before carrying Thomas back home. I softly kissed his forehead before laying him gently in his cot. I was relieved that he remained asleep, as I wasn't ready to attempt to explain why Tony wasn't in his bed. I just did not know how on earth I was going to explain to a two year old that his daddy had gone, and that he would never see him again!

The next day was the first day of December. As I lifted Thomas from his cot, I told him that it would soon be Christmas and that he could start opening the windows on his advent calendar. Once downstairs, he excitedly opened the first window and behind the little cardboard door was a star.

I picked him up and as I carried him towards the back door I attempted to explain why Tony wasn't in his bed. Due to all the excitement of the calendar, he hadn't actually noticed that Tony wasn't there; I think he just assumed that, like the previous day, he was still sleeping.

I just said the words, "Daddy has gone to heaven." Whatever that means, especially to a two year old! "And we won't be able to see him again... but at night when we look up at the sky we will see a big, big star and that's Daddy's star. Just like the one on your advent calendar."

As we both looked up together at the sky, the most amazing thing happened. It started to snow! I smiled and had a warm feeling in the pit of my stomach as I said, "Ah, look Thomas, Daddy has sent us some snow!"

Over 200 people attended Tony's funeral. The service was beautiful and very fitting. During the service we had the same reading that we had at our wedding, 1 Corinthians 13, and I asked Mike to play a recording of 'Fly' by Celine Dion. This was one of the songs on the album that I had played endlessly during Tony's illness and the words really resonated with me. I also wrote them on the card that was on the wreath from Thomas and me.

Tony was insistent on having 'Funeral for a Friend/Love

Lies Bleeding' by Elton John playing as his coffin was taken out of the church. This really worried me when he mentioned it in the months leading up to his death.

"You can't have that sort of music played at your funeral, Tony, it's not the done thing!" I would say, but he was determined and got quite angry at the thought of me not carrying out his wishes. I spoke to Mike about it on one occasion and he told me that Tony should have whatever he wanted.

However, I needn't have worried; his choice could not have been more perfect for me and for the congregation. Mike switched on the tape player and the haunting, instrumental music of 'Funeral for a Friend' filled the church. As the tune changed into the heavy rock sound of 'Love Lies Bleeding', the pallbearers began to carry Tony's coffin back down the aisle and I rose to follow behind with my family. We almost danced down the aisle, and my sister Tina shouted "Go for it Tone!" We left the church smiling and with happy memories of him, just as he would have wanted.

I had made the difficult decision to leave Thomas with a neighbour while we attended the funeral. I felt that he was too young to understand and I also needed to be with my own thoughts without worrying about him. As soon as we returned home from the church, I collected him from next door and as I took him through our back door he cried at the sight of so many strange people. Our house was jammed to the rafters with friends and family, leaving hardly any room for people to move. Suddenly, he set eyes on a familiar face and stretched out his arms to my mother.

Once everyone had left that evening, I felt exhausted and

numb. My mother and sister had decided to spend the night with Thomas and me, for which I was grateful. Since Tony had died, I hadn't been able to bring myself to sleep in our bed without him and had chosen to sleep on the sofa; that night was no different. As I settled into my makeshift bed, my mother and sister knelt down by me. Tina stroked my forehead as I cried tears of helplessness. I not only had both of them but also the rest of my family and friends; however, I still felt an immense loneliness and my heart was empty.

Tina spoke softly when she said, "I wish I could reach inside you and take away your pain." I feel sure that my sister and my mother were feeling even more helpless than me at that point, and probably wished they could be there for me every day.

"I don't know how I am going to do this alone," I cried.

Chapter Twenty-One

The days and months after Tony's passing, shall we say, passed! Despite my feelings of utter despair and devastation, I managed to dig deep and find many areas of my life to be thankful for.

I had my wonderful family and friends and Tony's parents giving me continuous love and support. My mother visited regularly and although my father was still living at the pub in Wales and I didn't see him much, he was on the other end of the phone.

I suppose one event that sums up my grief after Tony's death was when my mother and I went to the cinema to watch *Titanic*, which had been released around that time. During the film, I'm sure that just about everyone in the audience shed a tear at one point, and normally I would have been the first to blub, but on this occasion I didn't shed a single tear.

When the film ended, I remember feeling numb as I walked silently out of the auditorium with everyone else, as if I had forgotten how to feel any sort of emotion. The truth of it was that, at that moment, I didn't give a tinker's cuss about anyone else dying or anyone else's heartache; nothing could come anywhere near the pain and deep, deep sadness I was going through from losing my darling husband and father of my son. I asked myself if I was being selfish but decided that it was a self-preservation thing; I just did not have the strength or space in my heart to take on any more grief.

I was grateful to always have somewhere to run whenever I needed to, spending many mini breaks at my sister's house with her family. Thomas loved his Auntie Tina and Uncle Keith, as well as the company of his cousins, and I cherished the sibling moments with my sister. We all had lots of fun and I grew stronger each time we visited. Keith happily stepped in to take on the protective role for Thomas and me; he was the closest thing Thomas had to a daddy and was an excellent role model. Along with my mother and brother, we all went on holidays to EuroDisney and Center Parcs, where we had lots of fun as one big family. These times served as a welcome break for me, taking my mind off the huge, gaping hole in my life that Tony's death had left me with.

I was fortunate enough to not have to worry about finances, as Tony and I had been sensible with insurance cover. I was able to pay off the mortgage, and I also received a 'death in service' payment from Tony's employers. I was extremely grateful to not have to worry about making ends meet or having to go out to work when I was going through the process of grieving. It also gave me extreme pleasure to be able to treat my family, buying my brother a car and giving my sister and brother-in-law my car and some money, as their car had broken down on the day of Tony's funeral and they hadn't been able to get home. I also treated us all to holidays. For some reason, I didn't feel deserving of all the money and wanted to share it with the ones I loved and who had helped me.

Mike, the vicar, continued to pay us regular visits and it was on one of those visits that he brought a book for Thomas called *Water Bugs and Dragonflies: Explaining Death to Young Children* by Doris Stickney. It is the story of a colony of water bugs that couldn't understand why other members of the colony kept disappearing from the riverbed, never to return. One day, one of the water bugs climbs up the lily stalk, breaks through the surface of the water and falls onto a lily pad, where he eventually dries out and turns into a beautiful dragonfly; flying above the water, he tries to dive bomb the surface to get back to tell the others that he's okay, only to realise he can't. Not only is it a lovely story, but it also reminded Thomas of the time we went fishing with Tony and watched the dragonflies dancing on the water, making the sharing of the story even more special for us.

Tragically, six weeks after Tony's funeral, Mike had a massive heart attack while driving and died instantly. I was devastated by this news. He had been such a support to us all, and although the loss obviously didn't run as deep as Tony's did, it still hurt me very much and I missed his visits in the weeks that followed. Life could seem so cruel at times!

Four months after Tony's death, I held a memorial service for him at St. Lawrence Jewry church, by the Guildhall in London. This was mainly for his work colleagues who had remained at work whilst most of the other members of staff attended his funeral. Over 200 people attended, most of who joined us for drinks afterwards at a pub near St Mary le Bow, just off Cheapside; very near to where I first met Tony and where we spent many lunch breaks.

Above all else, the thing that made my life so much

happier and worth living at this time was being greeted by my darling little boy each morning. Getting out of bed and facing each day was made so much easier by Thomas's continuous happy disposition; not only that, he needed me, so I couldn't give up. If the truth were known, he was my saviour then and on many occasions in the years to follow. He was my reason!

All the time that Thomas was around me, I had him to focus on. He was a bundle of joy and energy and we would have fun, play and laugh, all of which didn't leave much time for sadness and grief. When he was at nursery school, I would fill my time with shopping or household chores. I found that as long as I was busy and occupied I was fine. My grieving process was to renovate and decorate the whole house; by the time I had finished, it was like a show home!

I was very much of the mind that I didn't want to bring other people down with my grief or make them feel uncomfortable, so I always put on a big, happy smile when I met friends, hiding the pain I was feeling inside. On rare occasions, the mask would slip as something would trigger my tears and there would be no holding them back. Obviously, everyone that ever saw this always showed absolute compassion, but I felt sorry for them, not knowing what they should do or say, so always tried hard not to let it happen.

I was soon to realise that this was a classic trait of mine; putting on a brave face when I was feeling wretched inside to protect the feelings of others. I also learnt that this could lead to further distress, which my body had its own way of dealing with in the form of a spontaneous eruption of tears.

My most challenging times were from early evening, when

Thomas was in bed, until I went to bed and finally managed to drift off to sleep. At first, it tended to go in fortnightly cycles. Something... or nothing... would trigger my tears and I would cry until I was too exhausted to cry anymore. In the few days that followed, I would feel lighter and able to smile more naturally, but then the emotions would start building again, like a lump rising up from the pit of my stomach. Sometimes, when it reached my throat, it would become stuck.

At these times, I would put Thomas to bed, pour a glass of wine, sit on the floor and listen to music; the music just engulfed me in thoughts of Tony, and I would sit with him in my thoughts and howl. Then the cycle would start again: I'd cope well for a few days, then not so well until... pow! The release valve erupted! This cycle went on for about five months or so, until my 'release' episodes started to become fewer and further apart.

The break in the cycle seemed to come when my parents, my brother, Thomas and I made a six-week trip to New Zealand with a three-day stopover in Singapore. As well as being a wonderful opportunity to see another part of our world, it gave me the chance to make the transition from being a married lady to being an independent lady who was entirely responsible for her life and that of her son. I returned home with a new perspective on life. Sometimes, by getting off the same old hamster wheel we get the chance to see life in a very different way.

Chapter Twenty-Two

In the two years after Tony's death, there were many happy times, many challenging times and lots of sad times, but life does go on and I believe it is in our nature to survive as best we can in whatever situation we find ourselves.

Thomas continued to be happy, funny and an absolute joy to have around. He never gave me a moment's grief and I still find it hard to believe that I had such an easy child. I feel sure that someone, somewhere was making sure that this was one area of my life that didn't throw me any curve balls during those difficult times. Tony was so right when he said that his 'bestest boy' would take care of me.

As Thomas grew older, I noticed lots of his daddy's characteristics in him: things that he could not have possibly learnt from Tony, as he was far too young. Yes, I could understand him having a similar personality like being kind, funny, happy, and never miserable, but Thomas also went on to have a love of the outdoors, nature and fishing, as well as a fascination with insects. He hated being cooped up indoors for too long.

Then there was the time when I was in the bath and Thomas needed to go for a 'poo poo', as he called it. He sat on the toilet happily chatting away and when he'd finished he reached for the toilet paper, saying, "Just three squares is all you need, Mummy."

I was speechless for a while as it took me back to Tony saying that to me in the bathroom the night before he died. There is no way that Thomas could have heard that comment, as apart from the fact that he was asleep in bed at the time, he was only out of nappies a few weeks prior to Tony's death and his daddy therefore never got the chance to do toilet duties.

On the first year anniversary of Tony's death, I put Thomas to bed, poured myself a glass of wine and sat on the floor to toast him and be grateful for how I had survived the year. I waited for exactly 6.30pm, the time of his last breath, and raised my glass, "Cheers my darling! May you continue to rest in peace."

As I put the glass to my lips I noticed that my hand was shaking and I was shivering with cold. I put this down to the emotions I was feeling as the heating was on full pelt, with it being November.

Ten minutes later, there was a tap on the door and I answered it to find Lorraine standing there in creased pyjamas. I was so pleased to see her and invited her in for a drink and to toast Tony. She was wearing the same pyjamas that she had been wearing one morning when Tony caught her taking the milk in on his way to work. He had wolf-whistled and they had laughed and joked like they always did. Since his death, she had found it too painful to get them out of the drawer and there they had remained until that evening.

"Blimey, it's freezing in 'ere!" she exclaimed as she walked into the lounge. "Why 'aven't you got ya heating on?"

"I have!" I said after going to check. It was on full blast, but there was definitely an icy chill in the room. I had felt it earlier and dismissed it, but now Lorraine was feeling it too. We both gave each other a knowing look as I said, "'Allo Tone! Have you come to visit?"

Soon after that anniversary was the second Christmas without Tony and my whole family were going to see in the New Year at the pub with my father. I decided to join them, but when it came to New Year's Eve I just couldn't face being at a party to celebrate another year without Tony, so I decided to drive home from Wales at lunchtime on New Year's Eve. It was very much a spur of the moment thing. I know the family were worried, but I knew it was what I had to do. I just wanted to be at home alone with Thomas and asleep when the New Year arrived.

As I expected, the roads where absolutely chock-a-block with cars full of families travelling to be with loved ones, and I knew the journey would probably take longer than usual; I was ready for a four- or five-hour trip. Thomas had fallen asleep in his car seat, which was in the front passenger seat of my Ford Puma. He had reached the age where he could be in his seat in the front, which meant I could keep a better eye on him and chat.

At one stage in the journey, while on the M4, there was a very short break in the constant three-lane flow of traffic and I found myself on the inside lane for the first time in ages. I could see three-lane traffic flowing in the distance, but the road immediately ahead of me was clear except for a car, which was travelling slower than me, in the middle lane. Rather than illegally undertake, I moved out behind it, at a safe distance, into the middle lane and then into the outside lane to overtake.

Just as I was coming up beside the car, it started to drift over into my lane and there was nowhere for me to go but towards the central reservation. It was too late for me to break or even to out-accelerate the other car. Then, to my absolute horror, I realised I was about to hit the barrier in the middle of the two carriageways, so I turned the wheel sharply to the left, at which point the car had got ahead of me, preventing me from crashing into it. Instead, the sharp action had made me lose control of my car and as Thomas and I spun around twice in the middle of the busy M4 motorway, the other car drove off into the distance, probably oblivious to what had happened.

Although this all happened in less than a minute, it seemed like slow motion to me. I held onto the wheel as the car spun out of control. I was disorientated, not knowing which way I was going, and I remember thinking, "Well there's nothing I can do now. How's this going to end?"

It ended with my car going up the grassy bank, rolling down again, on its wheels thankfully, and coming to a halt, half on the hard shoulder and half on the carriageway. As I looked up, I could see that we had stopped facing the oncoming traffic and the passenger door was in the direct line of the cars coming up on the inside lane. Thomas was in danger of being hit at any moment! In one swift move, I released his and my seat belts and dragged him from his seat, across my seat and out of the car through the driver's door.

Up until this point, Thomas had remained sleeping peacefully, for which I was so grateful; he hadn't experienced the car being out of control or seen the obvious fear on my face. Imagine his fear as he was awoken by me roughly dragging him out of the car and onto the bank of a noisy, cold and windy motorway. He let out the biggest scream I had ever heard from him and all I could do was hold him close to me, telling him everything was okay.

As I looked round, I saw a car had parked on the hard shoulder up ahead of us and a young lady was running towards us. When she reached us, I noticed that she was crying. "You're both okay! Thank God! My husband and I saw it all. Don't worry, it wasn't your fault!"

Her husband came to join us and they told me what they saw. The general consensus was that the driver of the other car had maybe drifted off to sleep for a second, as they saw them drift over towards my car and then suddenly right themselves and accelerate off. "You definitely had someone looking after you at that moment," the lady exclaimed. "When that happened there were no other cars around you, whereas the carriageway prior to and after that had been jam-packed with cars!"

An ambulance, which had been passing on the other carriageway when the accident happened, had taken the next exit to come back onto the motorway to check that we were okay. I took the names and address of the witnesses, and hugged and thanked them before they went on their way. Thomas and I sat in safety in the back of the ambulance until the police and later the recovery vehicle came.

One of the policemen commented that the type of car I had probably prevented us from rolling, due to its low-profile wheels, and that it quite possibly could have saved our lives, let alone allowing us to walk away without a scratch.

It took hours for us to get home in the recovery vehicle with my car on the back. Late that night, as I lay in bed, I was oblivious to the start of the New Year but yet again I had a strong feeling of Tony having been by Thomas's side and mine that day.

Chapter Twenty-Three

Due to the fact that Thomas was born in August, he had to start school when he was just four years and a month old. Although I thought he was too little, he did seem ready, having attended a Montessori nursery since just before his second birthday.

I had always been against sending him to nursery, which is why I left work when I had him, but Tony's illness had changed things. I hadn't been able to take Thomas out to toddler groups or to socialise with other children because I needed to be with Tony all the time. Realising this was an important part of his growth, I managed to get him a nursery place and it turned out to be the best thing. It was his bit of normality and routine in an otherwise hectic world at home, and it also prepared him well for starting school at a young age.

The day that he started at the little village school in Smeeth, near Ashford, goes down as one of the many times in his childhood that I wished Tony was there to share the moment. One of the hardest things about losing someone who was once in your life every day is not being able to share news with them at the end of each day. I wanted to tell Tony all about our little boy's first day at school, to share the pride, but I never could.

Thomas settled in very well and soon made friends, a few of which he used to have tea with at their homes after school. One day, I had gone to collect him from a friend's house, and as I stood in the kitchen with the other mother watching the two boys playing in the garden, I noticed that Thomas was riding a bike with no stabilisers.

"Oh my goodness!" I said. "Thomas is riding a bike with no stabilisers!"

"Yes," the other mother replied. "Did you not know he could ride a bike? He always does when he's here."

I was shocked and embarrassed but also saddened because during the time that he was at nursery, and while Tony was still alive, he was always asking me to take the stabilisers off his bike. I would explain to him that it's not that easy to learn to ride a bike and that I would have to spend some time teaching him. He would reply "But I can do it Mummy. It's okay." Tony's health then got worse and I never got round to teaching him. Thomas never asked again and continued to ride his bike, with stabilisers, around the cul-de-sac where we lived.

He had learnt to ride a bike at nursery school and I never even knew it. It obviously wasn't the great challenge I was making it out to be! I remember thinking this would have been one moment of pride I could have shared with Tony, if only I had believed Thomas, and for that I felt guilty.

It was around this time that my Financial Adviser, Clive, approached me about a job. He and some other colleagues had gone into partnership and set up a firm of Independent Financial Advisers. They were looking for someone to give them administrative support and he had thought of me, as my compliance training would come in very handy too.

Even though I didn't need to work from a financial standpoint, I was feeling a bit lost since Thomas had started in full-time education. The house had been renovated and decorated to within an inch of its life and took no time at all to keep clean, and there was the other issue of sometimes not having an adult to talk to for days on end. Added to that, I felt that the old grey matter needed exercising, so I decided to accept his proposal; however, it had to be on my terms. I wanted to be able to take Thomas to school, collect him and have the flexibility of being able to attend school events. So we agreed on me working from 9.30am to 3pm and only three days a week, which were flexible.

I was quite surprised by how good it felt to be wearing a suit again after just over four years away from the City. It's amazing how clothes can change how you feel; I went from being a mum back to being a professional businesswoman in an instant. I had loved every moment of being a mum, more than I ever enjoyed working, but it did feel good to have something to get my teeth into and to have more intellectual conversations again, rather than chats about what was happening in the lives of the Rugrats, the Bananas in Pyjamas, or Barney, the big purple dinosaur!

During my time in stockbroking, I sat and passed the Stock Exchange exams, which made me a representative of the Securities and Futures Authority (SFA) and licensed me to advise clients on the investment of stocks and shares. However, I chose to go with the compliance route, ensuring, among other things, that the fund managers and brokers were giving correct advice, that there was no insider dealing, that records and funds were being kept correctly, and that there was no fraudulent activity (i.e. money laundering); I found all this much more interesting than being a broker. To do this job you have to be registered with a company, so my registration lapsed when I left NatWest Stockbrokers to have Thomas. However, even if it hadn't, my qualification would not have allowed me to be an Independent Financial Adviser, as they deal with completely different products, for example mortgages, life insurance, critical illness cover.

One thing that did come in handy was my knowledge of compliance. Although I needed to learn new rules, the principle was the same and I had the mind of a Compliance Officer, which the Partners of The Pentagon Partnership appreciated very much. They trusted me to complete their administrative tasks well, with no corners being cut. They often said that they would have been hard-pressed to find another local person with my knowledge and expertise, plus I had the confidence needed to run the reception and to network at business events.

Chapter Twenty-Four

For the first time since Tony's death, I had started to feel 'normal' again. Thomas loved school and was getting on very well; I was enjoying working again; we had plenty of fun, family time; and, as finances weren't a problem for me, we managed to have plenty of treats.

There was one challenge, however. One of the Partners at work approached my desk one day to talk to me. "Alison, there's something I think you need to know as there may be times that you have to cover for me."

"Oh yes, what's that?" I questioned, intrigued as to what it could be.

"The situation is, my wife, Helen, is terminally ill and doesn't have long to live. She recovered from breast cancer five years ago but they have just discovered that she has a brain tumour." I gasped from the shock of hearing his news and all I could think of was that another young family was going to be destroyed. I told him that if there was ever anything I could do or if he just needed to talk to someone who totally understood, I was there for him.

After that, he did talk to me often about his wife and how difficult things were at home. Their two sons, aged seven and twelve, had not yet been told about the prognosis; they knew their mother was ill with cancer but didn't realise they were going to lose her soon. My heart went out to them all and I used to go home worrying about them. Not only that but it was bringing back the awful memories of Tony's suffering. Each day Barry was telling me how his wife was suffering, and it just brought all the sadness back for me.

One day, while Barry and I were chatting at my desk, I happened to mention that it was Sundays that I found the hardest. For the whole of my life Sunday had been a special day. As a child and teenager, we always had a family Sunday lunch, which would often be a two- or three-hour affair. Once I was married, Tony and I carried on with this tradition, although not for two or three hours, unless we had company.

Barry obviously went home and told Helen this as the next day he came into the office and asked if Thomas and I would like to go to their house for lunch the following Sunday. "Helen isn't well enough to cook and can't handle the smells, so I'm afraid you will have to put up with whatever I serve up! But you'd both be very welcome. It will be good for the boys to have some different company too," he said.

So the following Sunday, Thomas and I drove to Barry's house in Dover and I met Helen, Laurence and Alex for the first time. I found Helen to have a very warm, kind nature and she was very well spoken and articulate, which sometimes amused me when she spoke to the boys. I remember her saying to Laurence, while he was playing around with my video camera, "Have you noticed the effect that the light from the window has on the aperture, Laurence?" It just sounded so formal for a mother to be speaking to a child in that way: still, much better that way than the way some mothers speak to their children today!

Because of this, Laurence and Alex were polite, respectful and happy children. They loved playing with Thomas, who they thought was "Soooo cute!"

We had an enjoyable day and it was lovely to get to know Barry's family some more, although connecting with them made me feel even sadder for them all. Also, that day, when Laurence realised that Thomas's daddy had died from a brain tumour, he started to question whether that meant his mum was going to die too, and when she went upstairs he followed her to ask. Helen didn't lie and told him all she knew. Laurence came back downstairs with his mother much quieter than when he'd gone up, and snuggled up to her on the sofa for a while.

I felt very guilty that my being there had brought this on, but Helen told me later that she had been putting off telling them for a while, as she didn't know how to. She said I had made it easier as she could see, by looking at Thomas and me, that life goes on.

I was to spend many more lovely days with Barry and his family, including a trip to Walmer Castle when Helen felt well enough. On one occasion, they came to our house for tea and Helen spoke to me about her concerns for the boys when she was gone. She smiled as she told me of her worries about Barry managing to take care of the boys in the way they needed and joked that, after all, he was a man!

On a number of occasions she would say to me, "Thomas is a real credit to you, Alison. He is such a happy, polite little boy and you should be so proud of how you are raising him." I don't think she ever knew just how much her words meant to me at that time. One of the main things I worried about after Tony's death was how I was going to be a good mum and a good dad to Thomas.

I used to come home from seeing Helen feeling quite emotional but also very grateful for all I had. Here was this young lady of 42 (yes, the same age as Tony when he died) knowing that one day soon she was going to leave her young boys without a mother. The pain she must have been going through didn't bear thinking about!

Just a few months after I met Helen for the first time, she passed away in a hospice. Barry had called me earlier in the day to ask if I would drive over to Dover to look after the boys while he went to the hospice. Things weren't looking good at that time so the rest of her family were with her and therefore unable to have the boys. I took Laurence, Alex and Thomas to the seafront at Dover, as it was a lovely sunny day in August.

Unfortunately, Barry didn't make it in time and was told on arrival that Helen had passed away. Obviously, he was extremely upset about this and when he arrived back home told me that he felt so guilty for not being there. I told him that my belief, in these situations, is that those dying make a choice and that Helen didn't want the ones she cared about most seeing her at that stage. I didn't know what else to say to console him!

I attended Helen's funeral, standing at the back of the packed crematorium. My tears were not only for a mother having to leave her young sons, but also for a father left to pick up the pieces and the two young boys left to live a lifetime without their mother. It was heart breaking to watch this young family, knowing from experience exactly what they were now going to have to face.

Chapter Twenty-Five

Afew months after Helen's death, Barry approached me at work one day to ask if he could take me out to dinner one evening. He said he wanted to thank me for all the support I had given him and the boys during and since Helen's death, but also admitted that it would be good to get out and socialise for a change. I accepted, as I fully understood how he felt; the evenings are long when you no longer have your loved one around and it's good to have just one evening to take your mind off the loneliness.

We arranged for all three boys to spend the evening at my mother and father's house in Canterbury and booked a table nearby so that we could pick them up afterwards. I drove to Barry's in Dover and left my car; from there, we all went in his car over to Canterbury.

After dropping the boys off we made our way to the restaurant. As we were driving along a narrow and winding country road, a car appeared around the bend on the wrong side of the road. We slowed down to wait for him to move over, and when he didn't Barry made a quick decision to swerve to the wrong side of the road to avoid a head-on collision. The Lotus Esprit smashed head on into my door.

It was a bit of a rough impact but amazingly we were both

okay. We peered through the smashed glass of my side window to see the other driver slumped over his wheel. Barry got out and I climbed over to get out of the driver's door, as the other car was stopping me from getting out of my own. We spoke to the driver, asking if he was okay, but there was no reply. Barry called for the police and an ambulance and I called my parents to tell them what had happened, as we would need picking up once our car was recovered.

It turns out the other driver was released from hospital that night without any injuries, and it was suggested later that he was feigning being unconscious so as not to speak to us, maybe because he knew he was in the wrong. Apart from a bit of whiplash for me, Barry and I were okay.

When we got back to my parent's house, my mother recounted something that had happened to them that evening, which sent a chill down my spine. After we left to go to the restaurant, Alex had run out of the house and started chasing the car down the road. He was crying: "Come back Dad, I don't want you to go!" This was very out of character for Alex, as he was always a quiet, placid soul. Had he had forewarning of what was about to happen, I wonder?

We took a taxi back to Dover so that I could collect my car, but when we arrived back Barry asked if I wanted to have a coffee before leaving. He was well aware that the shock of the incident would probably set in soon and was worried about me driving home alone with Thomas. The boys went upstairs to play and Barry and I sat chatting about what had happened. Sure enough, the shock hit me like a lead balloon. I started to cry uncontrollably. "Barry, do you realise, all three of our boys could have been orphaned tonight?"

He put his arms around me and soothingly said, "I know, I know. But they weren't were they? We're both still here." It was so good to feel a man's strong arms around me again. I don't know if it was the shock of what had happened, the thought of not wanting to cope alone anymore through situations like this, or the need to rescue this man and be there for him and his boys, but at that moment I felt differently about Barry. He obviously felt something too because as I looked up at him he kissed me tenderly on the lips.

To cut a short story shorter, we got engaged on the following New Year's Eve, which happened to be the New Millennium, and we made plans to marry the following October. As two people whose spouses had both died when they were just 42 years old, we knew only too well how short life could be and we saw no point in waiting. It all seemed a bit like a fairy-tale and as if it was meant to be. I think we also believed after the accident that Tony and Helen were up there throwing us together... to support each other and to give the boys the normal family environment we both wanted for our children. Was it a match made in heaven?

It was all a bit of a whirlwind, really. We found an Edwardian five-storey townhouse in Dover and put in an offer, which was accepted. I put my house on the market and received three offers in the first week. The estate agents described it as the equivalent of a show home. The couple that bought it even bought all my dining room furniture, as they thought it suited the house perfectly. This was a godsend, as I didn't fancy having to move the marble dining table, which took four men to deliver.

I was able to buy the house in Dover outright with the proceeds from my house, but as it needed some work doing to it, I moved in with Barry and the boys until such a time as we could all move into the new house together. The three months that followed were very stressful for me. I spent the two days that I wasn't working, the weekends and some evenings working on our new home. Thomas was still at school near Ashford so I would take him and collect him on the days that I worked in the office, and Barry would take him on the other two days; however, I had to stop work at the house to collect him and it was an hour round trip.

Barry and Helen had both always worked since having the boys, so they had a lady who would collect Laurence and Alex from school and give them their dinner before Barry and Helen got home from work. Shirley had continued to work for Barry after Helen's death, and although I wasn't happy with a situation where the boys ate at a separate time to us, it was convenient for the time being and gave me one less thing to worry about. It also meant I could spend more hours working on our new home.

Eventually, I managed to get Thomas a place at a school in Dover, which made life much easier. However, moving him to another school so soon after he had started at his first school was traumatic for us both. He would be the only new boy, so it wasn't a case of them all being in the same boat. The other children were already settled and might not want a stranger joining them. I felt wretched on his first day and even he looked like he was going to cry, which wasn't like him. I hated myself for doing this to him and began to feel very selfish for deciding to uproot him so I could marry another man.

As I took him through the school gates, a little boy walked straight up to us and said, "Hello my name's David, what's yours?"

"Thomas," came the timid reply.

"Well, if you come with me I'll show you where you have to put your coat and book bag."

I was amazed at how grown up and kind this little boy was at six years old. Thomas looked at me for approval and I thanked David, kissed Thomas goodbye and left the school, crying all the way home!

The gratitude I felt for David remained with me for a long time and I was saddened to hear some years later that he had gone off the rails and started to get into trouble in and out of school. It seems he didn't have a happy, stable home life and I often thought of how different things would have been for him if he had. At six years old, he had the makings of a lovely young man, which were destroyed by his upbringing.

Barry's house eventually sold and we used some of this money for the work that needed doing on the house and to buy furnishings. The night before we were due to move into our new home, I felt physically sick with exhaustion and it was all I could do to climb the stairs to bed! My life had almost flipped on its head in the previous three months. I had gone from the peace and quiet of our home in Ashford since Tony's death, having only Thomas to take care of, to working long days into the evenings, seven days a week, decorating a five-storey house from top to bottom, getting to know my soon-to-be stepsons, taking care of three more people and supporting each of them through their own grieving process, when I was probably still grieving myself.

I had moved house just three months previously and was just about to move again, and I really didn't know how I was going to muster up the energy for the following day. I lay in bed, feeling very low and wondering if I was doing the right thing, but I put it down to tiredness and knew that it was too late now anyway since I had bought a house in Dover. If I'm honest, though, at that moment in time, the thought of going back to our simple, peaceful life in our lovely home in Ashford was very appealing.

Chapter Twenty-Six

We moved into our new home in the July. There were no carpets throughout the hall, stairs and landings, as I still had some decorating to do. It also made sense, as I had stored all the furniture from my house in the basement and it would now have to be taken up to each of the other four floors.

"Whose idea was it to buy a five-storey townhouse?" I commented to Barry as we carried one of the many heavy pieces of furniture from the ground floor to the attic.

The house was a real compromise for me. Barry wanted to live in the centre of Dover, not only because that's where he had lived since he was a child, but also because we were planning to start our own firm of Independent Financial Advisers working from home; this would enable me to work as well as be there for all three boys when they were home from school.

I have to say, the idea of just having to walk downstairs to the office every day appealed to me very much, after having commuted long hours in the past. Also, since leaving work to have Thomas six years previously, I had always been there for him and I wanted that to continue. However, I couldn't help feeling that living in the middle of town wasn't really for me. Having grown up in a village after leaving London as a four year old, I knew I was a country girl at heart.

Of all the places I had lived, I thought Dover town centre was by far the worst. I would leave our house, walk to the end of the road and cross over into the High Street, where many of the shops were empty or boarded up. The shops that were open consisted of mobile phone shops, charity shops and an amusements arcade. There were a couple of budget ladies clothes shops, which didn't appeal to me, let alone suit my shape, and there was absolutely nowhere to buy clothes for the boys. I would have to drive into Canterbury if I needed to buy clothes for any of us.

Worst of all was hearing parents 'effing and blinding' at their babies and children as I walked by; it was all I could do to not comment. For the first few months of living there, I used to get back home and want to cry, not only for those poor, innocent children but also at the thought of what I had brought Thomas to.

Prior to leaving our home in Ashford, Thomas had started to play out in our cul-de-sac. He made friends and they would play football, which he was becoming quite good at. At other times he would ride his bike or play in our sunny, south-facing back garden with Laura and another little girl from the close. All this ended when we moved to Dover. Our house was on a fairly busy road, where people used to park while shopping to avoid paying for a parking space in town. This meant that Thomas couldn't go out to play at all.

Our garden area was a very small courtyard on three levels, surrounded by other tall townhouses like ours. Years ago, all the gardens would have probably been one big communal one. There were a number of very tall trees in the gardens around us, which meant very little sunlight could filter through, making it a damp, mossy and slippery area. None of this made for a safe or easy place to play. Despite this, Thomas still managed to have fun collecting the insects and wildlife found under every damp rock in the garden!

The nearest park was a walk through the town, which I wasn't going to let a six year old do, especially with the type of people I was seeing out there every day. I soon realised that I would have to make regular trips to the seafront and parks with the boys so that they could get out to play.

However, Laurence and Alex were happier to play indoors, which may have had something to do with their father not rating football, or any form of exercise at all really. In the early days of me being with Barry, Thomas asked him if he could watch an Arsenal match on TV. "Why on earth do you want to watch a load of pansies running around after a ball?" was Barry's reply. Needless to say, Thomas didn't ask again. This really upset me and I told Barry so. Tony, who had once been a footballer and football coach, would have hugely encouraged Thomas's talent for kicking a ball.

Barry's main interest away from his work was politics. He had joined the Young Conservatives group in Dover when he was in his early twenties, prior to which, he told me, he was a bit of a loner. He always said that joining this group really brought him out of his shell, and helped him gain confidence. He made many friends and was later elected as a District Councillor, remaining one for some years.

In one way, Barry's love of politics was a godsend for me, as it put me in touch with many lovely people who, shall we say, were more like the people I was used to mixing with, having worked in the City and been brought up in a Conservative household. In another way, this love of his drove me to absolute distraction when he would get on his soapbox at some of our dinner parties and family get-togethers, bringing the good atmosphere to a sudden halt! When I was growing up, my father always used to say "Never talk politics at the table"—and I think he was right!

One of Barry's friends, who he met at the Young Conservatives as a young adult, was a lovely lady called Una. When I met her for the first time, she told me that Barry's late wife, Helen, had often talked to her about me, saying what a lovely lady I was and that she would get to meet me one day. Una didn't understand how she would get to meet me when I only worked with Barry in Ashford. She went on to become a very good friend of mine and has shown Thomas and me many kindnesses over the years.

Another friend was an elderly lady called Jean, who we often met up with as, like us and other members, she held regular coffee mornings to raise money for the Conservative Association. On my and Barry's wedding day, Jean came to me after the ceremony and said, "Alison, there is something that I have wanted to tell you and now is the right time. Helen said to me, when I saw her two weeks before she died, that she hoped you and Barry would one day marry, and here you are. A match made in heaven, I think."

Upon hearing this, I got goose bumps all over my body. So Helen, a dying mother worrying about her children's future, had chosen me to take over the role of mother to her boys... what a huge compliment! If I hadn't already felt a sense of responsibility for Laurence and Alex, I certainly did then.

Chapter Twenty-Seven

Our wedding day was a much larger affair than my two previous marriages. Barry and I felt that we wanted to extend a huge thank you to all the family and friends that had supported us both through the difficult times since the deaths of Tony and Helen.

We were married at 4.30pm in the ancient Stone Hall of Dover Town Hall. Earlier in the day I had set candles along every high window ledge in the hall so that we would be married by candlelight. The Town Hall was just opposite our road so we had no need for wedding cars. I had decided that Thomas should give me away, and as he and I stood behind the doors to the Town Hall, he looked down at the posy I was holding in my hands and said, "Mummy, you're shaking really badly! Are you okay?"

"Yes, darling, I'm fine. Are you okay?"

"I'm a bit frightened but I'm okay," he replied.

I wasn't really okay. I remember thinking back to the day when I stood at the end of the aisle with my father on the day I married Tony; I wasn't shaking then. I couldn't have been shaking because I was nervous. I didn't get nervous about things like that. The truth was that I, like Thomas, was frightened, but not about walking down the aisle among 200 guests; I was frightened about what the future was to hold. Life used to be so much easier when it was just Thomas and me. The previous months had left me feeling very weak.

Since moving in with Barry and his boys six months previously, everyday life had been a real challenge for me. Yes, I was exhausted from my extra workload of decorating the house in any spare moment I had, but I was also amazed by how hard it was learning to live with three new people who all had their own, different needs. As the lady of the house, it inevitably fell to me to support them, love them and sort out their problems.

Barry just wanted me by his side every minute that he wasn't working and would happily tell the boys to play in their bedrooms in the evening so that he and I could be alone in the lounge. I sometimes felt suffocated by this, but put it down to having to get used to having a man in my life again. I also didn't want to push any of the boys away; I wanted to live as a family. So, I had no 'me' time at all.

Barry was the first to admit that he wasn't the paternal type and he left it up to me, pretty much, to take care of disciplining, educating and occupying the boys. Helen's mother told me on many occasions that she thought I was sent from heaven to look after her grandsons and was always grateful for everything I did for the boys. Along with my mother, she was one of my biggest helps when it came to the boys; she was always available to talk to when I had concerns about either of them. She was very Victorian in her ways and I think the boys were slightly scared of her actions, so she was always my trump card. She also, understandably, liked to be kept 'in the know' about how her grandsons were getting on and treated Thomas as her own too.

One of the hardest things I have ever done in my life is take on someone else's children; they were good boys, and it could have been so much worse. However, they had both lost their mother at a very young age and their grief came out in different ways. I had to learn how to support each of them individually, without forgetting that Thomas needed me too.

Laurence was an angry teenager, who came over as very obnoxious and rude at times, quite possibly due to the devastating loss of his mother at a vulnerable age. But, if I'm honest, this didn't help me gel with him and made me more defiant towards him. I would never have been allowed to behave in the way he did, and it made it very hard for me to have empathy for him in his grief. I used to tell him that I had never made allowances for Thomas after Tony's death and I wasn't going to make them for him. I would explain that it's a difficult world out there and that no one else would make allowances for him losing his mother at a young age. Harsh, I know, but I couldn't let him use his mother's death as an excuse for his behaviour, as it wouldn't serve him well in the future.

Alex, on the other hand, was quiet and withdrawn at times and I worried about him more than I did Laurence. I understood, from my own experience, how holding onto your emotions gets the better of you sooner or later. The main problem I had with Alex was when he wouldn't eat his dinner. It took me a lot more time and effort to get him to eat more healthily, although, when I look back now, I realise how harsh I must have been. I'm pleased to say that he now eats anything and everything, and I think he's even grateful to me for persevering! It is so much harder to teach a child healthy eating habits when they haven't been instilled since they were a baby... I was changing a habit of a lifetime, but I believed that part of being a good mother was ensuring they ate healthily.

Laurence, being the outspoken one, demanded, and got, a lot of my time and energy; that's just what he needed. On many, many occasions, he and I would still be sitting at the table two hours after we'd finished dinner. There would probably have been an argument over dinner and I would then sit and try to sort things out with him. We nearly always left the table friends, but it left me mentally and physically drained, not to mention having to catch up with the chores that it had prevented me from doing.

I had to entice not only the boys but also Barry to eat healthy meals, as Thomas and I had always done, and this threw up some challenges. The lady that used to cook their meals had been told by Helen to grate vegetables into the boys' dinners so that they didn't know they were there. I was definitely not going to do this and I therefore had to treat them like young children, saying "I'll just put a little bit of each vegetable on your plate and you must eat it." I even had to do this with Barry, as he had previously mainly eaten microwave meals, and vegetables to him were peas and carrots only. Well, I didn't have to but I could not bring myself to give them unhealthy food and I certainly wasn't going to cook two different meals each night: one for them and the other for Thomas and me.

Barry and I honeymooned in Scotland. I hadn't wanted to travel far from the boys and wanted to know that we could get home at the drop of a hat if needed. One of the positive aspects of having been married before is that the boys had many sets of grandparents, who were all willing to take care of them whenever we needed them to. They all had a wonderful time while we were away.

We flew to Edinburgh, where we stayed for five days at Dalhousie Castle in Bonnyrigg, which is just 20 minutes from the city centre. The castle is steeped in history and we enjoyed nothing more than exploring the castle and learning about its past and the lives of those who had visited and occupied it since 1450, including royalty and ghosts!

We then hired a car for the remainder of our two-week stay and played it by ear from there, staying in hotels and B&Bs along our route. We took in many sights, including Fort William, Nairn, Ballater (home of Balmoral Castle), Dundee and much more. Of course, we just had to visit a whisky distillery while in the Highlands and chose Edradour, the smallest traditional distillery in Scotland. Edradour is like a 'model village', which is only home to people that work at the distillery and their families. It just so happens, much to Barry's delight, that they also supplied the House of Lords and the House of Commons with their whisky.

All in all, we had much-needed time on our own and returned home feeling refreshed.

Chapter Twenty-Eight

It didn't take long for the benefits of our break to wear off, for me anyway! Everyday life carried on like it had before, with all the normal challenges. On top of that, Barry and I were working on the set up and launch of our new business, which took up any spare time we may have had.

We launched the business in April 2001 with a drinks party at home for family, friends and networking colleagues. Barry had been a member of BNI, an international networking group, since being a founding member of the Canterbury branch in 1997, and we used to go to the weekly meetings every Friday morning, leaving home at 5.30am. I would be there most weeks as a substitute for members that could not attend for whatever reason.

Although it meant getting up at 4.30am every Friday, I always enjoyed the meetings, where I mixed with likeminded business people. I came away feeling invigorated every time. As for our own company, BNI accounted for about 85% of our business and not only did it give us an amazingly supportive network for business, it also led to many friendships and lots of socialising!

At about the same time as starting our business, I became Clerk to the Governors at Alex and Thomas's primary school, joined the Parent & Teacher's Association, and helped out at breakfast club. Working from home allowed me to get involved with these groups, and making friends with other parents gave me a very different form of socialising with our boys, as opposed to with Barry and the Conservative Association and BNI.

Life ticked along, albeit stressfully for me, and then in January 2002 another curve ball was to be thrown our way. My mother was diagnosed with breast cancer. She was 59 years old at this time, and other than that was fairly healthy. However, during the 10 years previous to that, she had been receiving treatment for pre-cancerous cervical cells and this gave us concerns that the cancer may have reached other parts of her body. We were all devastated by this news, but my mother took it very much in her stride. I'm sure that she was worried sick, but as always she was protecting her family by not showing it.

Thankfully, my father had returned home to Kent to live two years previous to this, after which they had moved from their large home with extensive gardens in Canterbury to a more compact house with a small garden in Deal. This was a great relief to my mother, as she no longer needed to find the time and energy to tend to the gardens and keep the large house clean and tidy at the same time as working long hours. She was working for an agency as a carer in the community, and was able to take time off work for her treatment and recovery.

In the March, she had a lumpectomy and her lymph nodes removed on the same side. Thankfully, the operation was a success and the cancer had not spread to any other areas. Obviously, I was very relieved by the positive results; the thought of not having my dear mother around filled me with dread!

However, the consultant stressed that they would need to give her a total hysterectomy as soon as possible after her breast operation. For reasons that I didn't understand at the time, my mother had been putting off having a hysterectomy, which had been suggested years earlier as a solution to the pre-cancerous cells.

I accompanied my mother to her check-up some months later. After examining her, the consultant said, "Right, Mrs Mills, now, about that hysterectomy. What about November?"

Before my mother had a chance to reply, I piped up, "Yes, that'll be fine, Doctor!" I just knew she was about to 'umm and ahh' with reasons as to why that wouldn't be suitable.

So, eight months after her breast operation, she underwent a total hysterectomy. It had been arranged that she would move in with my grandparents for the recovery period afterwards, as everyone knew that my father would not have the patience to take care of her needs, which would probably mean she would end up doing things around the house. Also, although my father had given up running the pub in Wales, he was still flitting back and forth for one reason or another, which was upsetting Mum enormously.

My grandparents did a wonderful job of looking after my mother and it was a special time for all of them. I don't think my mother relished the thought of her return home; she had got to rest completely for the first time in her adult life, not having to look after anyone but herself. I also think she knew that there were things she would have to face up to when she got home but really didn't want to!

The cracks were starting to show in my parent's relationship. My father's years away in Wales had not 'made the heart grow fonder', as my mother had hoped, and my father was obviously very unhappy at being back home with my mother, running back to Wales as often as he could.

Eventually, after much deliberation and many, many sleepless nights, the words 'If you love someone, set them free' seemed to resonate in my mother's head and she knew what she had to do, even if it was the last thing she personally wanted. She had loved my father all her adult life, and still did, in fact; the proof of that was that she was willing to let him go by placing his happiness over and above hers. She did exactly that.

One day, not long after she had returned home after recovering at my grandparents' house, she asked my father to sit down as she had something she wanted to say to him. Obviously, I will never know the words she said and I'm sure she doesn't remember them, but she told him that she wanted to separate, to go their separate ways and be happy. Knowing my mother, I am sure that everything she said was said in such a way as to not hurt my father in any way, even though at the time she had little reason to be that kind.

Chapter Twenty-Nine

It took nearly a year for the separation to be finalised and the house to be sold. My father bought a barn in France, which needed a huge amount of work to make it habitable. My mother moved to Dover, which was nearer to us.

The time leading up to their separation and the few years afterwards were challenging for the whole family, but I'm proud to say that our unconditional love for each other won out and no permanent damage was done to our strong bonds. Around the same time as receiving the news that my mother and father were separating, my life became even busier and hence more tiring and stressful in other ways, on top of the continuing challenges with the boys.

A good friend and his three older teenage children (two boys and a girl) were buying a house in our road, but their rental agreement came to an end prior to the house purchase going through. Me being me, I invited the four of them to move in with us until everything was settled.

They ended up staying for six months, which meant nine of us living in a four-bedroom house. I have to say, surprisingly, that I really enjoyed having them all to stay and so did our boys. It gave us some light-hearted relief, as they were a fun and happy family to have around. The boys all got on well and it was lovely for me to have a female in the house at last! It was school prom time for the daughter, so I really enjoyed going dress shopping with her and doing all those girly things. Most evenings, we would all eat together, sitting at the table for at least two hours with none of the usual arguments and upsets.

Among all the disarray in my life, I was determined to find something that took me away from the house and all its responsibilities. This ended up being in the form of French lessons at the local adult education centre in Dover. I had always been top of the class in French at school, and with my father living in France I felt that I had reason to pick it up again. I wanted to become fluent and this was made much easier with the opportunities we got to socialise with my father's French friends and neighbours during our visits to him. Those two hours a week were the only time I had entirely to myself and I loved it!

At the same time as having our friends living with us, I was training to become a Master Practitioner of Neuro Linguistic Programming (NLP). I had spent the weekend on a residential course; I clearly remember the Sunday evening when I returned after qualifying. Our friend's partner was visiting him and staying at ours for the weekend. She was in the kitchen doing some ironing when I got in and asked me how my weekend had gone.

"Oh, it was absolutely amazing!" I replied. "Although, I am utterly exhausted!"

I sat on the floor in the kitchen, leaning up against the cupboards, and I could hardly string two words together. My brain couldn't seem to find the words, and if it did I couldn't find the energy to pronounce them properly.

It wasn't long after this that our friends' house purchase completed and, I have to admit, however lovely it was to have them stay, I was grateful to see them go. I was exhausted and although I never had the house to myself, ever, it was good to not have so many people around to look after. This also made it easier for me to see my NLP clients from home, fitting them around my work commitments of supporting Barry in our main business. I would conduct consultations and sessions in the lounge of our house, two floors above where Barry was working, so it was very private and quiet. I loved being able to help others to transform their lives and had some amazing successes.

Unfortunately, within a few months of having some clients with quite traumatic problems, I realised that I was taking a lot of their negative energy on board and this, in turn, did not help my flagging energy levels. In my heart, I think I knew that I needed to do a lot more work on myself before I could help others.

Chapter Thirty

Giving up on my NLP business in no way stopped me. I always seemed to find something else to fill my time, usually in the form of helping or supporting others, in or out of the home. What I had learnt in all my training also served to help me understand and support the boys in a better way, so it wasn't wasted.

In 2004 Barry was elected as Chairman of the Dover and Deal Conservative Association and went on to serve for three years. This meant, among other things, that we seemed to have one event after another, including lunches and dinners with politicians, some of whom visited and even stayed at our house.

Oliver Letwin, who served as Member of Parliament for West Dorset, came to our house for pre-dinner drinks prior to us attending the Association Christmas Dinner at Dover College, a private day and boarding school opposite our house. I remember giving him a ticking off for feeding our dog titbits from the table!

Sir James Arbuthnot, Baron Arbuthnot of Edrom and Shadow Trade Secretary at the time, stayed with us overnight after being the speaker at one of our Association dinners. He was a very interesting man, born not far from us in Deal, whose company I enjoyed very much. He didn't like staying in hotels and was very grateful for us giving up our bedroom for the night, saying that it was more comfortable than a hotel anyway.

Then there was the time that I had to collect Ann Widdecombe, MP for Maidstone and the Weald from 1997 to 2010, from the railway station to take her to a lunch at the Churchill Hotel in Dover. A lovely lady, but let's just say she doesn't do small talk!

Obviously, it was a given that we would attend the Conservative conference each year and, on one such occasion, I think it was in Blackpool, I had James Landale, the Chief Political Correspondent for BBC News, shadow me for the day. He was doing a broadcast for Radio 4 and wanted to record my experience of and thoughts on the conference, as I was a young female who was quite new to the party conference scene. The broadcast aired the same evening.

This all kept me extremely busy, but I was very fortunate and felt enormously privileged to have had the opportunity to spend a week in France with my granddad, and many other Normandy veterans, for the 60th anniversary celebrations of the D-Day landings in June 2004. Throughout the week, we attended many memorial services where my granddad often recited the 'Ode of Remembrance', a verse taken from Laurence Binyon's poem, 'For the Fallen', which was first published in *The Times* in September 1914.

At the end of the week, heads of state and thousands of war veterans gathered to mark 60 years since the D-Day invasion of Nazi-occupied Europe. Queen Elizabeth was there along with 16 other leaders, including, for the first time, Russian and German heads of state.

The day spent at the British cemetery in Bayeux for the remembrance service, with our Queen, the Prime Minister, Tony Blair, and the French President, Mr Chirac, to name a few, was a long one for our veterans. They had had a long, tiring week and on this day they had to wait hours for President Chirac to arrive, as he was running late.

My grandfather stood for over four hours non-stop as there weren't enough chairs for all the veterans to sit. Being in his eighties, it wasn't comfortable for him to get down and sit on the grass. I remember thinking that 60 years on he was still as amazingly strong as he had been back in the war; I was so immensely proud of him.

Prior to the ceremony, I went and spoke to Michael Howard, who was Leader of the Conservative Party at the time. We talked for just a couple of minutes about politics and the fact that Barry was the Chairman of the Dover and Deal Association, but very soon the conversation got back to the veterans.

"So, what brings you here?" Michael asked me.

"My grandfather," I replied. "He's a Normandy veteran who landed a few days after D-Day and his mission was to head for Arnhem."

"Where is your grandfather now?" he asked.

"He's over there, shading under the trees," I replied.

"Please take me to him, I would love to meet him."

So I took Michael Howard to where my grandfather stood and introduced the two of them.

"It's a pleasure to meet you, Michael," my grandfather said as he shook the member of the Shadow Cabinet's hand.

"No, Bill, the pleasure is all mine!" he replied, and they

spoke some more about the struggles back then, which I will never, ever be able to fully appreciate.

My grandfather, Bill, was a Bombardier with the 94th Field Royal Artillery, part of the 43rd Wessex Division, and was based in Eastry, Kent prior to going to Normandy in June 1944. It was whilst he was in Eastry that he met my grandmother, Grace, at a tea dance in the village hall.

Their convoy went over to Normandy, arriving on 16th June, but was unable to land because of the bad weather. They spent three or four days on the ship, and, for the most part, Bill lay on his bunk feeling sick; the weather was so rough that the harbour was being broken up.

Finally, they were able to land and although their first objective was to capture the villages of Baron-sur-Odon, Fontaine-Étoupefour and Chateau de Fontaine and to recapture Hill 112, their main aim was to get to Arnhem. Operation Market Garden, which includes the Battle for Arnhem, was the largest airborne battle in history.

On 17th September 1944, thousands of paratroopers descended from the sky by parachute or glider up to 150km behind enemy lines. Their goal was to secure the bridges across the rivers in Holland so that the Allied army could advance rapidly northwards and turn right into the lowlands of Germany, hereby skirting around the Siegfried Line (the German defence line). If all went as planned, it should have ended the war by Christmas 1944.

Unfortunately, this daring plan didn't have the expected outcome. The bridge at Arnhem proved to be 'a bridge too far'. After 10 days of bitter fighting, the operation ended with the evacuation of the remainder of the 1st British Airborne

Division from the Arnhem area. However, although seen to be a failure at the time it later proved to be the beginning of the end of the war.

Bill and his comrades were in Bremen when the war in Europe finally ended on 8th May 1945, and one of their tasks included taking charge of Bergen-Belsen, a prisoner of war camp and a concentration camp, which was full of Poles, Czechs and other Eastern Europeans—all civilians who had been used as forced labour. The awful memories of entering Bergen-Belsen remained with Bill for the rest of his days and only once, during an interview that he did in his late eighties, did I hear him speak about it. At that time, he broke down in tears and had to leave the room.

Michael Howard told my grandfather about the members of his own family who had suffered at the hands of the Germans in a concentration camp.

To my amazement, a year later when Barry and I attended a private dinner with Michael Howard and about 15 other guests, Michael recognised me and straight away asked after my grandfather. I was astounded by his memory and his selfless concern for others.

Finally, President Chirac arrived in a helicopter and the proceedings got under way. After mentioning in his address that D-Day was for many of the veterans a harrowing day never to be forgotten, UK Chaplain General David Wilkes said, "There are some veterans in this service who remember because they cannot forget. Their lives were shattered by their experiences. We dare not forget."

By that evening, many of the veterans in our group were suffering with bad sunburn. By the end of the week, my grandfather had shed the top layer of skin on his face like a snake.

The day following the Bayeaux service, we attended the main international ceremony in Arromanches, where a warship fired a 21-gun salute. Veterans marched under sunny skies, past the Queen and many other dignitaries and leaders, to the strains of the theme music for the D-Day film *The Longest Day*. President Chirac decorated Allied veterans from across the world with the French Legion of Honour. The Arromanches parade by old soldiers, many of whom were in their eighties, was referred to by some as the Normandy Veterans' "farewell march-past".

About 250,000 died in the 80-day Battle for Normandy after 6 June 1944.

I was extremely humbled by the whole experience and so proud of my grandfather. I spent most of the week crying. When we arrived back in Dover, the first thing I noticed was a number of St George's flags being flown from the windows of houses. To my anger and distress, this wasn't in support of our D-Day veterans; it was in support of the UEFA football championships! At that moment, I knew that I could not allow Dover to forget the 60th anniversary of VE Day and decided to put on some sort of event in the following May to commemorate it.

Chapter Thirty-One

All in all, 2004 turned out to be another busy year for me. In the second half of the year, I became a school Governor at The Dover Grammar School for Boys, where I was later elected Vice Chairman of Governors. Alongside this, Barry and his politician colleagues somehow talked me into standing for election as a County Councillor, with the elections being the following May.

Although I didn't relish the extra work and responsibility, being a County Councillor would enable me to have some input into the education sector. I was particularly interested in the Healthy Schools initiative and, like Jamie Oliver, I wanted to make a difference.

Along with the other members of a six-strong committee, which I had set up after returning from France in the June, I was also working hard on the arrangements for a whole weekend of events in Dover to commemorate the 60th anniversary of VE Day.

This included filling the town's park and town centre with 1940s memorabilia and military vehicles; organising two full days of 1940s entertainment on the bandstand; arranging two evening dances, one in the Town Hall with a 16-piece big band and a team of Lindy hoppers, the other with a smaller band; organising a street party for about 200 children;

pulling off a march through the town to include veterans and the Parachute Regiment, which was stationed in Dover at the time; and arranging a memorial service on the Sunday morning.

I had to deal with all of this, on top of the everyday family challenges, with little or no support from Barry when it came to taking care of the boys and DIY jobs around the house. On one occasion, after a night out, I even found myself climbing into our en-suite bath while dressed in a long evening gown, having had a few glasses of wine. This was just to change the washer on the mixer tap, because Barry wanted to have a bath the next morning and I didn't want to get up early to do the work required.

By the end of the year I was beginning to feel like I had bitten off more than I could chew, as my health and state of mind seemed to be getting worse. I constantly felt like I was suffering from flu, with aching muscles and painful joints being the norm. I couldn't lie down or sit in the same position for more than five minutes at a time, as the pain on the pressure points was too unbearable.

As soon as I opened my eyes each morning, a feeling of darkness would come over me. Nothing inspired me to get up and I dreaded what the day had in store for me. I would feel groggy, as if I hadn't slept a wink when I had actually slept all night. I simply wanted to stop the world from spinning and get off. If it wasn't for the boys, I know I wouldn't have bothered to get out of my bed each day.

When I did get up, it sometimes took all my effort to get washed and dressed to see Laurence and Alex off to their school and to drive Thomas to his. Thomas's school was only a 20-minute walk away, but I never had the energy to walk him there, which filled me with tremendous guilt, as it would have been a good bit of exercise and fresh air for him before school. On many occasions, when I returned home from the 10-minute drive, I would collapse on the sofa and remain there all day, sleeping fitfully due to the aches and pains in my body. My concentration span and memory were so poor that I couldn't focus on reading a book or even watching a film.

However, I had far too many things that I needed to be getting on with so I had to battle through and force myself to carry on. Every now and then, it would all get too much and something, usually the smallest, silliest, most unimportant thing, would cause me to almost self-combust. I would turn into a monster, screaming at the top of my voice so that my throat hurt. Eventually, after exhausting myself, I would lie down on the bed or sofa, crying until I was too exhausted to continue.

Those times were starting to become more and more frequent, and, after one such episode, I lay in the foetal position on the chaise longue in the dining room, not an ounce of energy left in my body. For a while I was unable to move, talk or even cry.

The boys had been up in Laurence's attic room playing and probably oblivious to yet another of my rants. Barry was down in the office working. I wondered if they would even notice or care if I wasn't there anymore. I thought that Laurence and Alex in particular would be glad to see the back of their mad stepmother.

At that moment, my eyes fixed on the knife stand in the

kitchen, with its five shiny knives of assorted sizes sticking out of the wooden block. Without a second thought, I got up in a zombie-like state and started to walk over to the kitchen worktop and the knives.

All of a sudden, Thomas appeared from nowhere and cut across my path. It was as if I had zoned out completely, because I hadn't heard him running and jumping down the seven short flights of stairs from the attic, like he always did. As I looked down at him, it wasn't his head I saw on his shoulders, but Tony's face staring back at me. The sight stopped me dead in my tracks. I grabbed hold of Thomas and sobbed.

"What's the matter, Mummy?" he asked.

"Oh, nothing darling, I'm fine. Don't you worry about me. I love you so much!"

He cuddled me for a while, told me that he loved me and then asked what was for dinner. Satisfied with my reply, he ran back upstairs to join his brothers.

That was the moment that I knew I had to ask for help, for the first time in my life. How could I have EVER considered leaving my darling child without a father AND a mother, the child that had looked after me since the age of two and been my reason for carrying on in my darkest moments? I had to know why I had felt so ill for so long. I wanted to know how to sort it out, and I needed to know soon!

Chapter Thirty-Two

I made an appointment with our local GP's surgery and was asked which doctor I would like to see.

"I don't mind. I don't know any of them anyway as I never visit the doctor," I replied.

Up until that time, I had seen no point in going to see a doctor about my health issues, as I didn't think there would be anything he could do and believed he would probably just prescribe anti-depressants, which, for various reasons, I didn't want to take. The vast array of symptoms I was having included utter exhaustion, aches, pains, depression, mood swings, digestive problems, poor concentration, bad memory and sensitivity to light and noise, all of which caused irritability. All in all, I didn't really think the doctor would be able to help, but I was desperate.

After explaining how I had been feeling for the previous four years, which was getting progressively worse, I had some blood samples taken by the nurse and was asked to call the surgery for the results in a couple of weeks' time. When I did call, they asked me to make an appointment, as I needed to speak to the doctor about the results.

"Your blood results have shown that you have an underactive thyroid," the doctor explained.

"Oh, why do I have that?" I asked.

The doctor shrugged his shoulders and replied, very nonchalantly, "I dunno!"

I really wanted to say, 'And you don't care either, do you?' but refrained.

"So what does it mean?" I asked.

"Well, you will have to take thyroxine," he told me.

"For how long?" I asked.

"Forever!" was his reply.

I wasn't happy about this at all! I knew that just about every prescribed medicine on our planet could incur other problems or side effects. Since seeing what certain medicines had done to Tony's body, medicines that he didn't need to treat the cause of his illness but to counteract the effect of others, I had really hated taking anything, even aspirin. However, at that moment, I thought that if this was the reason I was feeling so ill all the time and if this medication could make me feel normal again, I would give it a try.

I went away and began taking the thyroxine, knowing that it would be a few weeks before I started to feel any improvements. In my heart, though, I felt sure that this wasn't the solution. I questioned why I had started to have an underactive thyroid at this stage in my life. I knew that it couldn't have come out of nowhere; there had to be a root cause.

After speaking to a friend about what the doctor had said, she recommended that I get a referral to an endocrinologist; this is a trained physician who specialises in diseases related to the glands. The diseases they are trained to treat often affect other parts of the body.

Well, this was easier said than done! The doctor had not

been very helpful and forthcoming with help or advice previously, and I was now questioning his expertise by asking for a second opinion; he wasn't happy! It took me weeks and numerous chasing phone calls to get a letter of referral, but I finally managed to get an appointment with an endocrinologist at the Chaucer Private Hospital in Canterbury.

Thankfully, I had private healthcare cover, as the blood tests and the consultant's fees came to over £600. The endocrinologist went into the history of my health in great detail, going right back to when I was a child.

A few weeks after my fairly traumatic birth, I had started to suffer from very bad infantile eczema, which continued until I was nearly a year old, at which time I had a bad bout of bronchitis. After that, I went on to be a fairly healthy, strong child, never really suffering from colds or stomach bugs.

After starting senior school at 11, I got quite heavily into sports, including athletics, netball, hockey and rounders. At the age of 13, I went down with glandular fever and all activities had to stop. I was doing a paper round at the time and after cycling around the village, carrying a heavy sack of papers each morning, I would sleep until the afternoon just to recover. Prior to going on holiday to Malta that year, I was told that I mustn't do any swimming. For someone so active, it was pretty grim and I struggled to rest.

I had a very healthy diet and my mother was a very good cook, serving up a wide variety of vegetables with meals throughout the week. We were also lucky enough to taste a vast range of dishes from other countries, as my mother had been introduced to many cultures while living and working in

London.

It was a rare thing to find sweets, crisps or fizzy drinks in the kitchen cupboards; this was a treat saved for Christmas and Easter. My father would, on the odd occasion, bring us home a 'finger of fudge' on a Friday evening, and I remember always being so happy about this; not for the chocolate but for the fact that my father had brought us home a treat. In a funny way, it made me feel special and loved. We certainly didn't feel hard done by because we didn't have sweets every day, or even every week, and this is, in fact, how I was with Thomas when he was growing up: sweets and fizzy drinks were a rare treat.

Unfortunately, my healthy habits started to take a battering when I left home at 19 to live in Southampton. I would never have breakfast before leaving for work in the morning, as I just couldn't face eating or even drinking at 5.30 in the morning. I would grab a toasted, buttered bagel and a cup of coffee on my way from the Underground station to the office, which I would eat at my desk before starting work.

By 11.30, I was hungry and would nip out to buy a large, cheese salad wholemeal bap or something similar. Sometimes I would also have a bag of crisps and a chocolate bar. Most lunchtimes I would go to a wine bar with colleagues and have one or two glasses of wine or gin and tonic.

I would get to Waterloo train station for my train home at about 5.45pm and the smell of warm pizza or hot sausage rolls filled the concourse. Knowing it would be about 8.30 in the evening before I served up dinner, I would buy a calorie-laden 'snack' to eat on the train with a cup of coffee.

Dinner would then be something quick, convenient and unhealthy from the freezer.

Things did improve slightly when I moved to Ashford with Tony, as I made more of an effort to prepare healthy meals. We bought a slow cooker and each evening I would prepare the meal for the next day, turning the slow cooker on before leaving for work. I would also cook healthy meals and soup in batches at the weekends and freeze them in separate containers. It helped that Tony was a healthy eater and loved his vegetables. We didn't own a microwave and reheated most of the things in the oven or a saucepan.

Getting the train from Cannon Street station meant there wasn't the temptation of hot food outlets, plus Tony wouldn't let me buy any snacks anyway. However, nothing changed with my breakfast or lunch choices, which weren't exactly healthy.

During the final five years of the 12 that I worked in the city, I was often signed off work due to exhaustion, which the doctor would put down to a virus, or 'yuppie flu', as it became known in the eighties and nineties.

I couldn't seem to find the time to exercise. A four-hour commute daily, leaving home at 6am and not getting home until 7 or 7.30 in the evening, and then preparing and eating dinner, didn't leave a lot of time to do much else. Weekends were taken up with food shopping, cooking, cleaning, washing and ironing and the odd bit of DIY and studying for stock exchange and compliance exams. To be honest, if I could find the time I wanted to just slump in a chair and do nothing.

So I suppose you could say that my lifestyle and the bad

habits I had got into during those years didn't help my health at all. I explained all this to the consultant and then told him about the stress and anxiety of taking care of my terminally ill husband, losing him, and re-marrying a widower and taking on stepchildren, as well as all the activities I was trying to fit into each day.

It was as if explaining all the events of my life, step-by-step, to another person brought about clarity. I felt like an outsider looking into another person's life and I could clearly see all the reasons for my health problems.

Two weeks later, I returned to the hospital to get the results of my blood tests. The consultant explained that they were all normal apart from the thyroid function. He said that my thyroid was slightly underactive but that this was just a symptom of an overriding condition.

That condition was Myalgic Encephalomyelitis (ME) or Chronic Fatigue Syndrome (CFS), as it later became known. He went on to explain that the condition is diagnosed by taking a detailed history and via the power of deduction when it comes to the blood tests. ME doesn't show up in the blood, and as there was nothing else untoward that could explain the reasons for my symptoms he diagnosed ME. This was based on my symptoms, my medical history and my lifestyle. He said that after what my body had endured since the age of 19, it was hardly surprising that I was suffering from the condition.

He told me to stop taking the thyroxine, as it was the last thing I needed, and added that there was no known cure for the condition; I would have to learn to live with it and manage my symptoms as best I could with a balance of rest and exercise and a healthy diet.

At the age of 36, there was no way I was prepared to feel like this for the rest of my life. Above all else, I wanted to be a fit, healthy and happy mother to Thomas. So I accepted the diagnosis in a positive light, glad that I now knew the reasons for my debilitating symptoms and that they didn't indicate anything terminal. I left the consultant's room determined to do whatever it took to recover from this condition.

Chapter Thirty-Three

One personality trait of mine, which I had started to become aware of, was that I always pushed myself to the limit; I was always fitting in one more job before going to bed. If I were decorating a room, I would work all day, often until 11 at night, without stopping for a drink, let alone something to eat. I almost felt guilty to just sit and 'be'. Once I'd started a task I found it hard to stop until I had finished it. I needed closure!

I also found it hard to say 'no' to other people's requests for help, helping out at every club or group whenever I was asked, and regretting it afterwards as it had added to my already heavy workload and stress. I wanted to rescue people and make their lives easier, like the time I invited our friend and his family to live with us!

I was always passionate about trying to 'sort' everyone out for what I thought was the better and tried to 'fix' people all the time. When it came to teaching my stepsons to eat healthy foods, to make conversation, to not use their mobile phone at the dinner table, to say please and thank you, and to get out in the fresh air to play, it almost became an obsession; I wanted to be the good mother that Helen, their mother, would have wanted for her children and I wanted to achieve it overnight! Of course, I also gave them love and plenty of attention as well.

Well, things had to change! It was 'me' that needed help now, more than ever; I needed to focus my determination, fight back for myself, and become 'obsessed' with getting 'me' well again. I had to put 'me' first and the boys a very close second; after all, if I didn't start looking after 'me', before everyone else, I wouldn't be able to take care of them. This was the only thought I needed, and it enabled me to not feel guilty about taking time out to rest.

Obviously, life still went on, I had responsibilities and couldn't make all the necessary changes overnight. There was the 'small' matter of my being a prospective County Councillor, with elections due in six months: the canvassing, the meetings at County Hall in Maidstone, the meetings and photo-shoots with visiting MPs, and much more.

As a founding member of the committee for the celebrations marking the 60th anniversary of VE Day in Dover, also happening in six months, I had many more tasks on my daily list: organising dignitaries to open various events during the weekend; planning and booking the whole weekend's entertainment; visiting the schools in Dover to talk about the children's street party; making and delivering over 200 ration cards for them to bring along; arranging caterers for the party food; arranging the memorial service and parade through the town; bringing together the veterans, the Parachute Regiment in Dover and various mayors from in and around Dover; applying for funding; and writing letters to local businesses asking for sponsorship. The list went on!

Added to that were my school Governor and school volunteer roles, as well as working in our own business for three days of the week, running the home and taking care of the three boys and Barry. I did what I could within those limitations and dropped my volunteering commitments at the breakfast club and the Parent and Teacher Association. I had no choice but to carry on with everything else, but I did work on making positive changes wherever I could.

I did some research into the condition, although I didn't feel I needed to know much more than the consultant had told me, and I certainly did not want to be told again that I had to live with it! I was interested to know, however, about the lives of others who had the condition because this would potentially show me what I needed to focus on first.

Myalgic Encephalomyelitis (ME) is a neurological condition that can cause long-term illness. No one person suffers in the exact same way and symptoms can fluctuate. Myalgic means muscle pain and inflammation, and Encephalomyelitis means inflammation of the brain and the spinal cord. It is sometimes referred to as Post-Viral Fatigue Syndrome (PVFS), as it can come about after the patient has had a virus.

Although the cause of the illness remains unknown, some experts believe it is triggered by a viral infection, such as tonsillitis, while others believe it is an autoimmune condition or metabolic disorder. In most cases, there seems to be a trigger and it is believed that certain factors can contribute to the development of ME – including emotional stress and traumatic life events, such as bereavement, as well as genetic susceptibility. Recurring viral and bacterial infections, stress and poor diet can worsen the symptoms of ME.

So that just about covered me; bronchitis, sporty and

athletic, glandular fever, recurrent viruses, divorce and bereavement, driven and enthusiastic, two car accidents, house moves, stepchildren, stress, poor diet during my late teens and early twenties. I'd been there, seen it, done it AND had the T-shirt.

In the past, people with this condition have been labelled lazy, but it appears to be quite the opposite, since ME tends to affect many people who are driven and enthusiastic, with high achievements and goals. Many athletes have been known to suffer from it. The fatigue experienced with this condition is very different from the everyday tiredness that we feel, say, from a long day at work, which for most people would be relieved by an early night. Sleep or rest does not relieve this type of fatigue.

Depression, mood swings and anxiety are all common side effects of the condition due to the many symptoms and significant lifestyle changes it can cause. Many people feel at a loss when it comes to leaving their old life or doing the things they used to be able to do. Sufferers often report problems with forgetfulness and struggle with the ability to find words, as well as memory loss and poor concentration. They can feel spaced out and disorientated, and can even have problems with coordination.

There are often issues with digestion, such as irritable bowel syndrome and a build-up of intolerances to certain foods, which the sufferer never experienced before. Sensory overload is also a problem for many sufferers; heightened awareness of noise and light can increase symptoms and irritability. A person talking at a normal level can be quite overwhelming for someone with ME. These problems can lead to a sufferer having to remain in a darkened room with no light or noise.

This is by no means an exhaustive list of the symptoms of ME, and I suffered with all of these, and more, over the years. Regardless of everything I read, I was sure that the ME was my body's way of telling me 'Enough now! I'm exhausted! What about me?' And that's when my journey of discovery and substantial learning began.

Chapter Thirty-Four

The first thing I did was to make it a priority to fit in some 'me time', and I don't mean flaking out on the sofa for hours when my body and my brain just couldn't take anymore, which had started to become a regular occurrence around my work. I started to have monthly reflexology treatments and massages, as this was a beneficial and therapeutic type of relaxation.

Whenever I felt strong enough, I would try to get some fresh air by taking a short walk. Thomas and I would get up earlier than usual and take a slow stroll to the seafront before getting ready for school and work. This always made Thomas's day; he loved being by the sea because it meant he could be close to nature and his beloved fish!

I enjoyed our moments together and found that they always lifted my mood, even if they didn't do my aching, painful limbs any good. Just getting away from the home environment, breathing in the fresh, sea air and being with Thomas, 'my reason', seemed to pep me up no end. He would chat away and make me laugh like he always had, and it made me realise how much I missed it being just him and me together; he was always a real tonic to have around.

I visited a naturopath who tested me for allergies and intolerances. Following this, I began to stick very rigidly to a diet that avoided all the foods that had become like poison to my body. I had a few sessions of colonic hydrotherapy, which had an amazing effect on my bowel habits. Since I was a very young child, I had been prone to constipation. I even remember an occasion when I was in the bathroom of our home in London, with my mother and father, while my sister was downstairs enjoying her birthday party with friends. My father had to give me a suppository to help me go to the toilet, as I would cry from the pain of not having been for days.

Without going into the gory details of my sessions with the retired nurse who performed the colonic, I found it weirdly satisfying to see the waste matter that came out of me. The nurse explained that it had been like layers of woodchip wallpaper lining my bowel and intestines, for what was probably years. This would not only have led to toxins leaking into my bloodstream, but it would have prevented my bowel and intestines from pulsating and contracting, as they should have. This meant they hadn't been able to move waste through and out of my body effectively.

Prior to having my first session, I was advised to start taking probiotics, as the treatment would stir up all the old waste and could lead to other problems. I continued to take probiotics for many years after this, to keep my gut healthy, and I found them to be a great help with my irritable bowel-type symptoms.

My Neuro Linguistic Programming (NLP) training gave me all the tools I needed to stick to my new eating regime and to think positively whenever I had a 'crash'; this is the term used when sufferers have a relapse and their conditions worsen, usually when they have pushed themselves too hard and failed to strike the right balance between rest and exercise. I also noticed that it wasn't just physical exertion that put a strain on my energy levels but mental exertion too, so I would try not to do too much of both on the same day.

Everything was a fine balance and I wasn't very good at getting it right to start with, especially with my continuing workload. I remember thinking to myself on many occasions, 'My thirties have been shit but my forties will be fabulous!'

At that time, those were pretty much the only things I managed to change with life being so hectic. The normal, as well as different, challenges with Laurence had continued throughout the years. As he got older, he became more argumentative and arrogant. By this time he was 18 years old, which made things much harder for us both. There was no way he was going to listen to me or accept any guidance or advice I gave now that he was a 'man'!

Not only did he look down on me physically, at 6ft 2 inches tall he towered over my 5ft 4-inch frame, but also mentally... it was as if I was something he had scraped off his shoe. He would often comment that he could move out at any time, as his friend's mother had offered him a bed at their house. He was still at school, completing his second year of sixth form. Although the thought of him no longer disrupting the household seemed pleasing, I still cared about him and his wellbeing and needed to know that someone was keeping an eye on him. I didn't want him going off the rails at such a vulnerable age, so this for me was not an option.

Most of my and Barry's arguments were centred on Laurence and what I felt was Barry's lack of support for me in this area. I was at the end of my tether and would often cry myself to sleep after discussing it with him yet again and feeling like I'd achieved nothing. I just didn't know what to suggest; fatherhood didn't seem to come naturally to Barry, and it wasn't something I could teach him.

One time, I suggested that he make a point of taking the boys out for the day, once a month on a Saturday or a Sunday. This would give me a bit of 'me time' with the house completely to myself, which never happened and would have been bliss, as well as potentially helping Barry and the boys to 'bond' a bit more. I think he did this once and then never again. If we went out, it was as a family and only because I had arranged it.

Eventually, I made the very difficult decision to step back and not discipline or try to guide Laurence anymore, to try not to care about and even ignore what he did or didn't do. As a mother, this was a massive challenge because you can't just stop caring! I informed Barry of my decision and said that he would have to keep an eye on him to make sure he was safe and wasn't getting into anything he shouldn't. I also told him that if he cared about Laurence's exam results, he would need to check that he was completing his homework. This had always been my role with the boys and, like most boys, they always needed a 'kick up the backside', metaphorically speaking, to get going on their schoolwork.

Two weeks after Barry and I had this conversation, Barry had been reprimanding Laurence for something and Laurence responded by calling him a "bastard". I don't think I had ever seen Barry so angry. His face was red with rage and I really thought he was going to hit him, but I think he knew that if he did he would do some real damage. His reaction was to tell Laurence to leave and move in with his friend, as he had kept threatening to do for the previous few months.

I supported Barry's actions wholeheartedly. Laurence could not continue to behave in the way he had, disrupting the whole household and getting away with it. I in no way wanted Thomas to think he could behave in such a way either. I knew, as Barry did, that Laurence had somewhere safe to go. Barry wasn't throwing him out on the streets.

We had met the friend's mother on a number of occasions and she was okay, even if Laurence had got dangerously drunk at the age of 16 while in her care! On this occasion, I slept in the lounge on one sofa while Laurence slept on the other, as I was fearful of him choking on his own vomit. Our bedroom was in the basement and Laurence's was five floors up in the attic. I would never have slept for worry. Barry's reaction was, "Oh, he'll be okay, don't worry!"

I may have supported Barry's actions but I did find it ironic that after just two weeks of me turning the responsibility for his care over to Barry, he'd been thrown out! I'm happy to say that after just four days, Laurence popped home to see us. He and I sat on the basement stairs in our bedroom talking for some time, while Barry worked in the office. He apologised to me, for all the hurt he'd caused and his arrogant attitude, saying "I had it coming to me and I deserved all I got."

Bless his heart! I'm not sure he did deserve all he got but I was so proud of him and grateful for what he said. Since the death of his mother and my marriage to his father, things had not been easy for him. I always tried to understand that, but would never accept the arrogance. After all, it was just as difficult for Alex and he didn't behave in such a way.

Laurence never did move back home. He stayed at his friend's until such a time as they both got jobs after leaving school and could afford to rent a flat in the town. If the truth were known, he couldn't wait to get out from under his friend's mother's roof either! He came into his own when he got a job, started paying bills and running his own home, and I am very proud of the man that he has grown into.

Chapter Thirty-Five

So, with Laurence gone, life became slightly less stressful for me but, due to my commitments, I couldn't totally rest in the way I needed to and I was constantly fighting the various symptoms of ME and regular 'crashes' where I would take to my bed or the sofa for a day or more.

In the February of 2005, it all became too much and I felt I needed to run away. I knew I was going to struggle to get through the following months with the County Council elections and the VE weekend celebrations, and decided I needed a holiday before it all really kicked off!

Of course, there was no way I was going to 'run away' without Thomas, 'my reason' and the one person in my life that seemed to give me extra energy, happiness and positivity whenever he was by my side. I was desperate for some quality time with my son. I was constantly aware that he wasn't getting as much of my time as I would have liked and I wanted to make up for it.

Thomas was getting on very well at school and I felt that 'time out' at this point in his education, while he was still in junior school, wouldn't be to his detriment; I would never have considered taking him out during term time when he got to senior school. So, I asked for permission from his headmaster, who agreed based on the fact that both my life and Thomas's had been very stressful since the death of Tony, which had been just over seven years previously.

I didn't tell Thomas beforehand, and as soon as I had discussed it with Barry and got the 'okay' from the school I booked a two-week holiday to Lanzarote. It was last minute and therefore very inexpensive, and I could almost guarantee good weather. As soon as I clicked the 'Book Now' button on the computer, it was like a lead weight had been lifted from my shoulders. I couldn't wait to pick Thomas up from school to tell him the news.

"Hi sweetheart, did you have a good day?" I asked him at the gate. It always filled me with joy, seeing him bound out of school with his book bag and a huge grin on his face!

"Yes. Mummy, can I have Shaun and Thomas round for tea tonight?"

"No, not tonight darling, I've got a lot to do." I replied, watching the corners of his mouth drop.

"Ohhhhhh! Please! We won't get in your way."

"No, I'm sorry Thomas but I have to get on with some packing as you and I are going on holiday!"

"Really? When?" he shouted with delight.

"The day after tomorrow, so you better get your skates on!"

"Oh wow! That's what I love about you Mum, you're crazy and fun!"

Crazy... yep, that just about described me in a nutshell, but not in the way he meant!

He gave me a huge hug and said "Thank you! Thank you! Thank you!" Of course, on the way home from school that day

Thomas asked one question after another and I got so much pleasure at being able to give him this opportunity. I was happy and excited but that feeling soon diminished when I had to tell Alex that I wasn't taking him.

Understandably, it was really hard for him to see why he couldn't be taken out of school at this stage in his education; he was 14 years old and therefore preparing for his GCSEs. I felt very sad for him and extremely guilty, but I needed this break so much and I couldn't expect Barry to take care of Thomas while I was away. I told him that we would go away somewhere in the UK during the summer holidays, since I knew that money wouldn't stretch to a holiday abroad for four during the school holidays.

The next evening, we had a huge dumping of snow and I was very concerned over whether or not we would be able to make it in time for our very early flight. I hated driving in snow and ice and knew that we would have to leave at a stupid hour to make sure we arrived at Gatwick on time. Thankfully, I discovered that friends of ours were also flying to Lanzarote that day and they offered to give Thomas and me a lift to the airport.

The next morning at 3.30 when we left, the side roads were pretty treacherous where the snow had iced over in the night, but the motorways were fairly clear, albeit only one lane at times. We arrived safely and in plenty of time for our flight, and Thomas and I enjoyed a breakfast in the airport terminal. I felt liberated and so happy to be spending time with just Thomas. Much to our relief, our flight took off on time despite the terrible weather conditions.

As we walked down the aeroplane steps at Arrecife airport,

under the blue, cloudless skies, the warm air hit our faces. Even the familiar smell of diesel was a comfort to me, reminding me of the many previous times I had flown to hot countries for a holiday.

After collecting our cases from the carousel, we took a bus from outside the airport to our destination. We stayed in a small apartment complex just outside the town of Costa Tequise but within easy walking distance of the beach, restaurants and shops. We had a small communal swimming pool and bar area, and because it was term time it wasn't overrun with other children. This didn't bother Thomas, as he was happy to spend time with me.

I bought him an inflatable dolphin, which he named 'Dauphin', the French term for the species. He spent hours playing in the pool on Dauphin while I sunbathed and read a novel for the first time in years. Both of us did an introductory course in scuba diving in the pool; however, Thomas was too young to do a dive in the sea and I wouldn't leave him to do it on my own. I promised him that we would do it when he was old enough, perhaps in the Maldives where his daddy and I spent our honeymoon.

On most days we would go to the beach, as this was where Thomas preferred to be. He spent hours climbing on the rocks and watching the fishermen catching fish on the jetty. He was never happier than when he was by the water and fish! I bought him a net and bucket so that he could catch all sorts of marine life, and I taught him how to snorkel. In the evenings, we would find a good, authentic restaurant and Thomas would eat lots of different foods that he hadn't tried before. We would sit and talk about the day we'd just had and what we planned to do the next day.

On one of the days, the friends who gave us a lift to the airport and who were staying in Playa Blanca drove over to take us out for the day. We visited many places, including Jameos del Agua, an area formed out of spectacular volcanic eruptions from the volcanic mountain Volcán de la Corona, which formed huge subterranean tubes and caves all the way down to the ocean.

Inside the caves is a subterranean lake, which has salty but very clear water. Here, tiny, white and blind crabs can be found. These crabs normally live in deep seas of more than 2,000 metres in depth. The level of the lake depends on the different tides of the ocean, which cause water to filter through the volcanic tunnels and caves. There is also a subterranean auditorium, which is a fantastic volcanic cave where approximately 600 people can enjoy marvellous natural acoustics in the form of concerts, ballets and other cultural activities.

Thomas and I really enjoyed our visit to other parts of the island, but were relieved to get back to the swimming pool to cool off. It was hard to believe that we had left a snow and ice covered UK and after just a four-hour flight were in temperatures of 26 degrees Celsius and more.

All in all, we had a very enjoyable time, which was extremely relaxing for me too. I was able to rest all day, get plenty of fresh air and sunshine, completely shut off from any stresses or worries, spend quality time with Thomas, and even be in bed by about 9.30, all of which was just what I needed.

It was, however, a real shock to my system when we

arrived back home to reality where, funnily enough, nothing had changed and the benefits of my break were soon lost.

Chapter Thirty-Six

The weeks and months that followed were occupied with working in our office, taking care of Barry, the children and the home, leafleting and door-to-door canvassing for the elections, preparing for the VE Day celebrations, doing school Governor work, and training for my NLP Master Practitioner certification. That's not to mention meetings, meetings and more meetings!

By the time voting day for the Kent County Council elections arrived on Thursday 5th May 2005, it was all I could do to put one foot in front of the other and string two words together. To this day, I really don't know how my body kept going. It was as if I had two targets to hit: the elections and the VE Day celebrations. I was like a heat-seeking missile locked on to these targets; nothing would sway me off track.

I had been working almost non-stop for the previous couple of months and I was starting to worry about what the extra workload would do to my physical and mental health if I were to be elected as a County Councillor. Worse still, I didn't want to let down the residents of Dover Town when they had put their faith in me.

Having said that, the day and night of Election Day were surprisingly exciting and exhilarating for me. I spent the whole day visiting the various polling stations in the Dover

Town area for which I was standing for election, and at about eight in the evening Barry and I popped home for some dinner before walking to the Town Hall later that evening for the count.

Not only did we have a Labour Government at that time, but Dover Town was also a Labour stronghold, with the two available seats being held by the party. I was one of two Conservative candidates, standing against the two existing Labour Councillors and two Liberal Democrat candidates. Although it seemed unlikely for us to gain both seats, it wasn't unachievable. Perhaps the normal Labour voters had become complacent and not bothered to turn out to vote! We hoped to gain at least one seat.

The other Conservative Councillor was already a District Councillor and well known in the town; I, on the other hand, was new to the scene and had had to work very hard, in the months leading up to the election, to get myself and the principles I stood by known. So, it was an amazing experience for me to see piles of voting slips where the Dover public had actually put a cross next to my name!

I chatted to the two Labour Councillors, who I had known for some time. I saw one of them regularly at our local residents and neighbourhood watch meetings, and we always got on very well. It never mattered to me what side of the political fence they were on; they, like me, just wanted to do the best for the people of the town. In my eyes, that made us equal.

When the time came, in the early hours of Friday morning, for Nadeem Aziz, the Deputy Returning Officer, to announce the results, I felt nervous and excited all at once. All six of us candidates stood in line on the stage waiting for the results, which, if I remember rightly, were read out in alphabetical order of our last names.

Collor	Conservative Party Candidate	3,455
Hook	Liberal Democrat Candidate	2,658
Mackie	Liberal Democrat Candidate	2,255
Newman	Labour Party Candidate	6,194
Sansum	Labour Party Candidate	5,888
Williams (me)	Conservative Party Candidate	3,122

Neither of us Conservative candidates won a seat that night, but for me personally the whole experience was one that I learnt so much from. I met some very interesting people and got to know and understand more about the challenges of everyday folk and politics. I also felt extremely chuffed with the amount of votes I had received considering I was an unknown candidate in a Labour stronghold.

The Labour Party, under Tony Blair, won its third consecutive victory that year; however, the seats they held were reduced from 160 to only 66. Tony Blair returned as Prime Minister, with Labour having 355 MPs and a popular vote of 35.2%, which was the lowest proportion of any majority government in British history. In terms of votes, they were only narrowly ahead of the Conservatives but still had a comfortable lead in terms of seats. The Conservatives had 198 MPs, 32 more than they had previously, and won the popular vote in England, still ending up with 91 fewer MPs in England than Labour. The Liberal Democrats saw their popular vote increase by 3.7% and won the most seats of any third party since 1923, with 62 MPs.

Almost as soon as the results were out, I went home, ate some breakfast and grabbed a couple of hours' sleep. The two-day VE Day celebratory event was to begin at 9.30 the following morning, with the Mayor of Dover opening the event on the park bandstand. However, there was still a huge amount of organising to do before then and I needed to be there.

I felt like a zombie when my alarm went off mid-way through the morning and it took all my effort to get out of bed, have a quick wash and walk to the park. There was already a huge amount of activity going on and I got on with putting up our tents and gazebos with the help of the other committee members.

I was there all day setting up, and that evening we sat in the park eating fish and chips with some of the military vehicle owners, cadets and 1940s enthusiasts who were camping there all weekend. Even though we had provided security fencing, security guards and guard dogs, the 1940s vehicles and equipment were all very valuable, in both monetary and sentimental terms. I don't blame the owners for not wanting to leave them overnight. We were all exhausted but excited at the prospect of how the weekend would pan out.

When I got home that Friday night, I remember thinking, as I turned out the light, what a mad couple of days it had been, in which I had only had about four hours' sleep. I can only assume it was the adrenalin that was keeping me going and it reminded me of how I existed on such little sleep during the weeks leading up to Tony's death. I fell asleep as soon as my head hit the pillow.

Chapter Thirty-Seven

My alarm woke me on the Saturday morning at 6am and I jumped out of bed, again due to adrenalin but also excitement and the thought that I needed to be in the park to organise the arrival of more vehicles and traders.

I showered and dressed in my borrowed authentic 1940s-style army uniform, which consisted of a straight army-green skirt and smart jacket, a beige shirt and a brown tie. The look was completed with skin-tone, seamed, silk stockings and flat brown lace-up shoes. I put my hair up in a 'victory roll', on top of which I placed my cap. A victory roll was a woman's hairstyle that was popular in the 1940s, named after the aerobatic manoeuvre and World War II support efforts in general.

When I went into the kitchen, I found Barry looking smart in his 1940s army officer's uniform and Thomas dressed as an evacuee, wearing grey flannel shorts, a white shirt and grey tank top, grey knee-length socks and black plimsolls. I had made him a box to hang around his neck, which back in the day would have contained his gas mask. At the age of nine and three quarters, it had been a bit of a challenge to get him to dress like this, but he was doing it for his Grandad Bill! There were also going to be many other children, including his best friend Thomas, whose mother Sue was on our committee, dressed in a similar way. I didn't even try to get Alex to dress up. At the age of 13, that just wasn't cool!

As we needed to get to the park early, we decided not to stop at home for breakfast but to have a bacon roll and a cup of tea from one of the catering vans in the park. I could then eat and organise at the same time!

I have to say, when I think back to the VE Day celebration weekend now, a lot of the detail is a blur to me. I was running on autopilot for much of the time; I just got on with what was required, and now don't remember what I did. There was so much to do and think about, and I, and the rest of the committee, just didn't stop from dawn to dusk on the Friday, Saturday and Sunday! Thankfully, my very good friends Una and Sue were part of the committee and this made the stress of organising things so much easier to handle, as we all knew each other and got on well. If we felt like screaming, we could and none of us would bat an eyelid!

My overriding memory is that the whole weekend was a huge success; the weather was very kind to us, with no rain and warm sunshine. The park and town centre were both full of people who had come to enjoy the celebrations, and I felt that we succeeded in educating the younger folk a little bit more about what the people of the 1940s endured for our freedom. We were able to show our gratitude to the veterans that attended and, more than anything else, I was so happy that my grandfather was there with us to enjoy it all.

It was a free event for all as we had managed to get lottery funding on the basis that the whole event would be educational, especially for the school children, who were by that time starting to learn about the Second World War in their history lessons. Much to my, Una's and Sue's delight, we were very lucky to have the support of an army of muscly Paras, from the 1st Battalion Parachute Regiment, who were stationed in Dover at the time, along with the local air cadets. They all helped with the set up on the Friday and were around to assist for most of the weekend, even having to put up with a load of middle-aged women lusting after them!

Members of the public were able to wander around freely, looking at 1940s vehicles and watching re-enactments of the Home Front and displays by the local air cadets, as well as shopping at the many stalls selling 1940s clothing and memorabilia. There was an original 1940s NAAFI (Navy, Army and Air Force Institutes) food wagon onsite, selling tea, coffee and all types of authentic cuisine from the era, including bread pudding, which was my grandfather's favourite. We even had vintage fairground rides for the younger children to have some fun.

Men dressed as 'Spivs' roamed the area trying to sell their American silk stockings. The word 'spiv' is slang for a type of petty criminal who deals in illicit and typically black-market goods. The word was particularly used during the Second World War, and in the post-war period when many goods were rationed due to shortages.

A troupe of Lindy hoppers provided the audience with regular dance displays around the bandstand. The Lindy hop is an American dance that emerged in Harlem, New York City, in the 1920s and 1930s, and originally evolved with the jazz music of the time. It was very popular during the swing era of the late 1930s and early 1940s, and was a fusion of many dances that preceded it or were popular during its development. It is mainly based on jazz, tap, breakaway and Charleston. It is frequently described as a jazz dance and is a member of the swing dance family.

All in all, the first day was a huge success, with hundreds of people filling the park for most of the day. We closed the gates to the public and, after clearing up, the committee all rushed home at about 6pm to get changed ready for that evening's entertainment.

Chapter Thirty-Eight

We had organised a ticket-only dance at Dover Town Hall, which thankfully was at the end of the road where we lived, as I didn't have much time to get washed, changed and over there to meet the band when they arrived.

A few of us had managed to get into the Town Hall on the Friday, as soon as it had been cleared after the election count, to put up bunting and flags and decorate the tables with everything red, white and blue. It seemed a bit surreal to me at the time. One minute I was in the Town Hall standing up on stage awaiting the results of the 2005 General Election, and a few hours later I was decorating the hall 1940s-style to celebrate the end of the Second World War!

I also found it weird that the previous year, when I returned home with the veterans from the D-Day anniversary celebrations, the day that I decided to put on this event, was also the same day as the European Elections and I spent that whole night at the count in the Town Hall too.

As soon as I got home from the park, I went straight to our bedroom, had a quick wash and made an attempt to apply some 1940s-style makeup. This was easy, since in those days makeup was hard to come by and therefore minimal. I then donned the 1940s vintage evening dress that I had hired previously. Thankfully, when I let my hair down from its victory roll I had an abundance of soft curls, which framed my face perfectly, meaning that all I needed to do was put an authentic-looking hairpiece in place and 'Bob's your uncle'; I was good to go after only half an hour!

As I arrived at the Town Hall, the band members were already unloading their instruments from the coach at the main door. I introduced myself to the bandleader, who I had only previously spoken to by phone, and then let them get on with setting up.

Prior to the guests arriving, I stood with my grandfather at the back of the Maison Dieu Hall, within Dover Town Hall, while the band tuned up. They were The Jeff Short Swing Band, a Big Band consisting of 16 musicians playing four saxophones, four trombones, four trumpets, piano, bass and drums, plus vocals. All of a sudden, the band launched into playing 'In the Mood' by Glenn Miller and my grandfather and I got goose bumps. The sound coming from the stage across the high-ceilinged dance floor was absolutely amazing and took our breath away.

Sixty years previously, the Dover public would have been celebrating the end of the war in this very hall and listening to the very same music. Victory in Europe Day, generally known as VE Day, was the public holiday celebrated on 8th May 1945 (or 7th May in Commonwealth realms) to mark the formal acceptance by the Allies of World War II of Nazi Germany's unconditional surrender of its armed forces. It thus marked the end of World War II in Europe.

As I turned to my grandfather with tears in my eyes, I noticed that his face was crumbling too. We hugged and

I said, "This is all for you Grandad! Enjoy! And thank you for all that you did for us back then."

I later looked on proudly as my grandfather 'whisked' my grandmother around the entire outside of the large dance floor; they still had it even though they were in their eighties. In my eyes, they owned the floor that night! I imagined them doing the same dance back when they first met at the tea dance in Eastry village hall. I had never been taught to ballroom dance properly, but under the guiding hand of my grandfather I always managed to get it close enough. I still treasure those special moments when I got to waltz with him.

The evening was a huge success. We organised a raffle and raised a fabulous amount of money, which went to the British Legion. People talked about it for a long time afterwards, all saying how rare it was in this day and age to be able to listen and dance to a 16-piece Big Band in such an impressive venue.

The Sunday was yet another full day of events, with more of the same from the day before along with some added extras. The main ones were a march by the veterans, Paras and cadets, a memorial service and a children's street party in Dover's Market Square.

In the morning, my grandfather led the march followed by a few remaining Normandy veterans and Market Garden veterans, some of the Paras, and the air cadets and their band. I could not have been more proud of my grandfather as he marched through the town right up to the memorial in front of Maison Dieu House in Dover and saluted; he stood tall, proud and strong, dressed in his blazer adorned with many medals and wearing his army beret with his regiment badge. I knew that, if nothing else, all the blood, sweat and tears that had gone into organising this weekend had been worth it and nothing like what he had endured when fighting for our country!

Members of the public followed the parade through the town and joined in with the memorial service, which was conducted by the then-vicar of St Mary's Church in Dover Town, the Reverend David Ridley. At the eleventh hour there was a two-minute silence, and I fought back tears as I thought of all those that had lost their lives fighting for our freedom. At the same time, I felt grateful that my grandfather had not been one of them. Also in attendance were a few local dignitaries who joined our committee members, the veterans and the Paras for tea and biscuits in the Mayor's Parlour after the service.

At lunchtime, we had over 200 children from various schools in Dover join together for a replication of a VE Day street party. They each received their own ration card and ate only food that would have been around during rationing times, such as egg sandwiches, jam sandwiches, spam sandwiches and rock buns.

Throughout the whole weekend, there was back-to-back entertainment on the bandstand in the park and one of our acts were the wonderful Swingtime Sweethearts, two lovely ladies and successful solo artists whose affection for the forties brought them together. They sang a wide range of songs from the 1940s, both wartime and swing, including the hits of The Andrew Sisters, Vera Lynn, Anne Shelton, Gracie Fields and Glenn Miller.

We had arranged a Vera Lynn lookalike and it was an

emotional moment for me when I saw my grandfather, adorned in his medals and slightly bent over with fatigue by this time, chatting to 'Vera Lynn' by the bandstand as the Swingtime Sweethearts belted out 'There'll be Bluebirds over the White Cliffs of Dover' and 'We'll Meet Again'. I, along with my grandfather, grandmother and Barry, had been fortunate enough to attend a dinner with the real Vera Lynn, and her daughter, only a few weeks prior to this.

During the weekend, I was to feel a whole bundle of emotions – pride for my grandfather for what he had gone through and how he had survived and continued to live life with an almost permanent smile and constant friendly, cheeky banter; grateful that he was there to see everyone's gratitude for what he and his comrades endured; and happy that I had made the decision nearly a year previously, upon returning from the D-Day celebrations with the veterans, to organise this event. It had been a massive challenge for me with my energy levels so low, but I remember thinking that it was nothing compared to the challenges that my grandfather and many thousands of other men and women experienced during the war. It was the least we could do in remembrance of them all.

As the final day of celebrations came to a close and I and the other organisers began the big clear up, we felt exhausted but elated. It had all been a massive success and I don't know whether it was the extreme joy of the moment or that we had just gone plain mad, but we all decided to do it again the following year!

Chapter Thirty-Nine

A month later, close to my 38th birthday, I went away for the weekend to complete my NLP Master Practitioner course and certification. It was an amazing and very enlightening experience, and one in which I learnt a lot about myself.

I felt as though I was going home a changed woman, having had many 'Aha' moments, but to say that I came back down with a bump would be an understatement. It was as if as soon as I was able to give up the fight, I did, well and truly! My energy levels hit rock bottom, and for a couple of days I actually didn't get out of bed. When I eventually did, I spent days on the sofa. I didn't want to move or speak. I was in a lot of pain constantly, and had to change position every 10 minutes or so to ease the pressure on my aching muscles and joints. I couldn't concentrate on the TV or read anything. I felt numb and very, very low.

However, the training I received had confirmed in so many ways what I already knew but didn't always put into practice; I must take responsibility for my own life and the only one that could get me out of this mess was me. I had made decisions, or lived my life in a way that had become detrimental to my wellbeing, and I needed to re-evaluate everything that wasn't serving me well.

I had been brought up with my father saying, "You make your bed, you lie on it!" and to a certain extent I agree with this. I agree that we pay the price for any decisions we make, but on the other hand I believe that we make choices based on the knowledge, beliefs and needs that we, or others, have at the time. I have always considered how my decisions will affect others but have not always realised how they could end up being to my detriment, therefore putting others' needs before my own.

If it turns out, later down the line, that your choice has become detrimental to your wellbeing, I believe you CAN and must make changes! I'm not only talking about making changes in relationships here. You may also need to look at any bad habits you have, the type of work you do, the people you socialise with, the type of exercise you do, the food and drink you consume, whether you get enough rest – the list goes on!

I had been told, and agree with, that there is no medical cure for ME, and anyway the last thing my body needed was to be pumped full of prescribed medicines from a doctor. What I did believe was that I could recover by making huge lifestyle changes. After all, I believed it was my lifestyle that had got me in that state in the first place.

The NLP course had helped me to understand how my past actions and behaviours, and even my personality traits, had led me to this condition and now I had the knowledge and tools to change those patterns. I knew that the ME was my body's way of saying 'What about me?' So what about me? What was I going to do to get 'me' better?

After just over a week of rest and thinking about what

I was going to do to move forward and become stronger, I began to feel as if I was back in the land of the living. I knew that I needed to take drastic action with my lifestyle if I was to have any chance of recovering from this condition; it wasn't going to just go away but I always believed I would beat it. I had to beat it... my son needed me!

I was fortunate in that a huge amount of my previous workload and commitments had ended. At that moment, I was immensely grateful that I hadn't been elected as County Councillor, that studying for my NLP course had ended, and that the VE celebrations were over. It was a great weight off my shoulders, but it wasn't enough.

I had to go right back to basics. I decided I would do only the absolute necessities, for a while anyway. I would get out of bed each day, drive Thomas to school, walk to the shops, buy the ingredients for a healthy meal, prepare a healthy meal, and work in our office only when I needed to. On the days that I didn't need to work, I would rest or go for some sort of holistic therapeutic treatment.

Barry had decided to make some changes in the business, meaning that for a while he wasn't able to give financial advice, which meant my administrative tasks lessened. This also meant we had little or no income for a year. We had to take out a mortgage on our home to cover the cost of living during this time. It wasn't a nice feeling, knowing that I had been mortgage-free since Tony's death and that we were now having to start borrowing on the house that I had bought for cash. However, Barry convinced me that the changes in the business would be for the better, so I agreed.

At this time, I was grateful for the monthly annuity I

received from Tony's mis-sold pension, as this enabled me to pay for treatments, vital nutritional supplements and anything Thomas needed without feeling guilty. I knew Tony would have approved of how I was spending that money at the time, and Thomas never went without the necessities in life.

I cancelled all social events at home and away from home and didn't plan anymore for the foreseeable future. I resigned as Vice Chairman of the school Governors, and ended all my voluntary commitments and my French lessons. As well as regular visits from my mother, my friend Una would also come to visit; it was always lovely to have another understanding female to chat to.

I have to say, after getting over the guilt of feeling like I was letting a lot of people and organisations down, it felt like a huge weight had lifted from my body and my mind. Although to start with I struggled to do even the most basic of tasks, within just three weeks I felt a lot better. I continued with the healthy eating regime that I had begun after I was diagnosed with ME and in fact became even stricter, as I had the time to prepare a wider variety of healthy meals. I wasn't doing any socialising either, which had often made it a challenge to stick to healthy choices in the past.

I didn't push myself physically at first, only having very short walks to start with, usually to the shops to get food. However, as the weeks went on I became stronger and started walking again with Thomas to the beach on some mornings. I had more time generally to spend with Thomas and Alex, even if it was only for indoor activities at first.

I was really pleased when Ian, a friend and a really kind

and gentle ex-military man, took Thomas under his wing and regularly took him fishing. I will always be grateful to Ian for taking the time to enable Thomas to get out of the house when I couldn't, and for encouraging his already keen interest in fishing and nature, which was something Tony would have done if he were around.

Thomas would help Ian clear the River Dour in Dover, loving every moment of being among the fish, insects and ducks! Ian and his family even took Thomas with them to the Army and Navy rugby match at Twickenham on two occasions. This was the closest Thomas got to a normal father/son relationship and Ian was an excellent mentor, which made me very happy.

Sometimes, when I felt a bit stronger, I became tempted by requests for help from others and constantly battled with the issue of saying 'no' to people. It was always a fine balance, but in time I learnt to listen to my body and got to know 'me' very well. I kept reminding myself: 'My thirties have been shit but my forties will be fab!

Chapter Forty

I suppose it was around this time that I started to notice the lack of synergy in my relationship with Barry. Prior to this I hadn't really had time to think about it. Ever since the day when I first met his terminally ill wife, Helen, and his boys, I had somehow just wanted to help and even take care of them all, and I did just that. From the moment I moved in with them, my feet didn't seem to touch the ground. I just got on with the job of being wife to Barry and mother to all three boys, along with work and all the other everyday chores

Barry was 12 years my senior, the same as Tony was, but unlike my relationship with Tony, the age difference seemed to be more obvious with Barry. Barry was kind, loyal and an excellent businessman, but I couldn't think of a single interest that we shared, apart from eating out at restaurants. He only ever really talked about his work and politics, didn't really seem to enjoy travel or socialising, unless it was a Conservative Association event, and he wasn't a one to bother about visiting family unless I suggested it. By contrast, I loved socialising, meeting different people, having our extended family and friends round to dinner, dancing, music, travel... the list goes on! He also left the care and discipline of his boys completely up to me, never really getting involved unless I begged for support.

Our relationship was a challenge from day to day. I was becoming more and more unhappy and unfulfilled and started to question what had attracted me to Barry in the first place. Had there been some sort of heavenly being directing me to this path? Was taking care of him and his boys another of my purposes in life, I wondered? However, I knew that there wasn't anything I could do about it; I had our children's feelings to think about, not just Barry's and mine.

As I grew stronger, my need to escape from home and everything that went on there grew. Unfortunately, Thomas was at senior school by then and there was no way I would take him out to go away on holiday. Aside from that, funds wouldn't stretch to holidays at that time. My father was still in the process of converting his barn in France, which at times was a lonely and tiresome task for him. At the same time, I was feeling the need to be with my daddy... the man who understood me and just 'got me' more than any other man!

So, whenever I could get a Ryanair return flight for £40 or less, from London Stansted to Limoges, I would up and go for a week. It was easy to catch up on work in the office, as there wasn't much to do at that time, and Thomas and Alex pretty much looked after themselves, with Barry providing takeaways or microwave meals for them each day. I knew that a week of unhealthy eating every now and then wouldn't hurt!

I loved being in France with my father and I always seemed to come alive and feel much healthier and fitter when I visited, even though I was working hard on the barn while I was there! I had no responsibilities and it was a very, very relaxing place to be. We would sleep and eat in the static mobile home that my father had sited behind the barn, which he was occupying until his new home was habitable. Our day would start at about 8am, when we would have a quick breakfast before getting on with whatever tasks needed to be done.

When my father purchased the barn, it was an old, dilapidated, stone-built building in the middle of a wild meadow. Cows had been kept in the barn and would have grazed on the surrounding land. The area that was later to become his kitchen still had layers of cow dung and mud on the ground, and it took my father, and a friend, weeks to clear it and dig down. Apart from the rickety mezzanine floor above this part of the barn, there were no other partitions and the barn was an empty, draughty shell with holes in the roof and walls, which allowed all sorts of wildlife in to nest.

My father worked tirelessly on the renovation for four years, having occasional help from friends, family and tradesmen for all the jobs that he wasn't qualified to do, like building the new roof, electrics and gas. When I was there, I turned my hand to all manner of jobs, including preparing the stone walls for pointing by using a pick to clear hundreds of years' worth of mud, dung and dirt from in-between each stone. I spent nearly a whole week doing this, perched on scaffolding right up in the dizzy heights of the barn roof. During the final stages of the work, I tiled the kitchen floor, the shower room floor, the kitchen walls and worktops, and cleaned the oak beams with wire wool before applying linseed oil.

My father had rules, which he knew he had to adhere to; otherwise he would have burnt out before the end of the project. There's a lesson I wish I'd learnt from him in my younger years! Rule number one was to down tools for an hour at midday to eat lunch. In the winter, this would usually mean eating homemade soup and bread while thawing out our hands and feet by the heater in the mobile home. In the summer, we would eat bread, cheese, pate and salad at the table in the garden under the warm sun or in the shade if it was too hot! Then we'd get back to work until 4pm, at which point rule number two would come into force. We would down tools for the day and head to Les Bruyères, a family-run bar and restaurant in the nearest village, Cussac, which was a 10-minute drive away.

I loved to sit at the bar, drinking a kir (white wine and cassis) or two, chatting away in French to Fernand, the owner, Agnes, the waitress, and the other locals who had popped in for a drink after work prior to going home to their families and dinner. Not only was there always lots of fun and laughter to be had, but I was also getting the practice I needed with my French speaking. Occasionally, my father and I would eat lunch at Fernand's; an amazing four-course 'menu du jour' of home-cooked food prepared by his wife, Celange, plus half a carafe of 'vin rouge', could be had for just 10 Euros.

I would often chat to my father's doctor, who was a Chinese Frenchman and well trained in many Eastern therapies and medicines. One day, I was telling him, in French, about the symptoms I had been suffering as a result of ME and he told me to pop over to his surgery before I went home, so that he could give me an acupuncture treatment. Looking back on this after sometime, I believe that the treatment almost certainly had a positive impact on my energy levels and aching muscles. However, I was unable to keep up with the treatments since poor Dr Chan passed away not long after.

I enjoyed my regular visits to France, not only because they allowed me to escape my unhappy everyday life, but also because they gave me the opportunity to spend special, quality time with my father, which was priceless. Interestingly, even though I was working physically, and was constantly on the go at my father's, I only ever felt a healthy, natural tiredness at the end of each day and awoke feeling refreshed every morning. This was as opposed to the extreme exhaustion and the aching muscles and joints that were constantly apparent when I was at home.

Over the following two years, I continued to make regular trips to France. In the summer months we would drive down as a family and spend two weeks with my father. Thomas loved the fact that he could fish in the large lake at the bottom of his grandfather's garden at any time of day or night. He was in his absolute element when among nature and all things slimy and crawly. Even Alex had begun to appreciate the outdoors more, and the two of them would spend hours looking for creatures to collect in jars and tubs, which would be found all around the barn.

I continued to battle with my energy levels, aches and pains, and occasional low moods during these two years. My health was a bit like a rollercoaster, up and down all the time, but with every 'up' I seemed to achieve that little bit more and be better than the last up; with each 'down', I didn't seem to get as low and would recover quicker. So, I always saw improvement, which gave me hope and the willpower to keep up the good habits.

Chapter Forty-One

When it came to my 40th year, I was determined to enjoy the whole weekend of my birthday, no matter what my energy levels were at that time. I would just have to pay for it afterwards!

I decided I wanted to throw a party to celebrate. After all, it was to be the beginning of the rest of my life! Barry commented that we couldn't afford a party and my reaction was, "Don't worry, I WILL have a celebration and I will cover the cost myself!" I was determined to mark this pivotal point in my life. My 30th birthday party had been a bittersweet affair. With Tony having just finished his radiotherapy treatment, all we could think about was what was to come. I wanted to see all the friends that my busy life had not allowed me to see for years.

By this time, I wasn't having as many energy crashes. I was feeling stronger, but not as strong as I should have been. I still felt vulnerable and was easily affected by the stresses of life. The flu-like muscle and joint aches weren't as debilitating but were still there; at least I was now able to lift my arms to blow dry my hair without having to lower them for a rest every few seconds, and it was no longer a strain to hold my hands up at the ten to two position on the steering wheel. My mood was still quite low most of the time, but the thought of a party with lots of my old friends and family present kept me upbeat and positive.

I had a wonderful birthday weekend. On the Friday evening, my actual birthday, we enjoyed a dinner with family and some close friends at Blakes in Castle Street, Dover. The food was delicious and the company entertaining. Not only did Tony's mother and father, Hazel and Terry, come, but his aunt and uncle, Keith and Barbara, travelled all the way from Cornwall. This was a real treat, as I hadn't seen them for quite a few years. It was also very lovely for Thomas to see some of his daddy's family again.

On the Saturday evening, I had a party at the Bluebirds venue, close to the marina in Dover; another 100 people or so came along. There were friends there from when I worked in the City and even a school friend who I hadn't seen for 20-odd years. The following day, a few of us went out for Sunday lunch in a nearby village.

All in all, my birthday celebrations were just as I would have liked and a very positive start to my forties! In fact, from that weekend on, a lot seemed to change for me as regards my health and wellbeing. I had started drinking Aloe Vera Gel a few weeks previously, on a daily basis, and this seemed to be helping many of my symptoms, so much so that I felt strong enough to start building up from the yoga stretches I had been doing to a more strenuous form of exercise.

I bought a mini trampoline, put together a playlist on my iPod and every morning I did half an hour of rebounding, which is bouncing up and down on a mini trampoline, doing various steps and arm movements. I would then end the session with some yoga stretches.

I had no trouble getting out of bed each day, not having that black mood upon waking that I had had for years but feeling totally refreshed after a good night's sleep. I was sticking to a very healthy diet, and was even able to do an extreme juice detox for a week to find nothing but beneficial effects.

Apart from making me fitter, stronger and more toned, all of this led to me starting to shed the excess weight I had been carrying for years, and in just six months I had lost about three stones in weight. I felt great and from that moment I never looked back as far as my energy levels were concerned. I was just continuing with the good habits I had got into over the previous three years, but for some reason everything had clicked into place and was making me feel better.

I started to wonder if this was proof of what having a positive mental attitude could do for you. For approximately two years prior to my birthday, I had often said to myself 'My thirties were shit but my forties will be fab!' I only wish I'd said to myself 'In six months' time I will be fit, healthy and full of energy!' I could have got to this stage much sooner!

Unfortunately, things weren't getting any easier in our marriage. Alex was nearing 18 and we hardly saw him. He was either out with friends, climbing a mountain, or doing something similar! He had joined the Combined Cadet Force when he was at school, which turned out to be the making of him. After leaving school he found a job locally but continued with many activities, mostly to raise money for charity, including doing a long walk in aid of Help for Heroes, climbing Mount Kilimanjaro and doing the International Four Day Nijmegen March. He was very into his music, teaching himself to play guitar and later becoming part of a band. He had grown into a fine young man and I was very, very proud of him. That left just Barry, Thomas and me at home for the most part. Barry's behaviour often led me to believe that he felt Thomas was in the way, now that both his boys weren't around.

One day, in the March of my 42nd year, something happened between Barry, Thomas and me that turned out to be the straw that broke the camel's back. I had bought some Hot Cross Buns as a treat for the weekend and on the Sunday evening as Barry, Thomas and I sat watching T.V., I asked if anyone would like one. Both Barry and Thomas said they would, so I went down to the kitchen to get them. To my surprise, there were only two buns left and I wondered how because neither Thomas nor I had eaten any and I had bought eight only the previous day.

I went upstairs with the two remaining buns and asked Barry whether he had eaten any over the weekend, to which he answered that he had and when I questioned how many, he said that he couldn't remember. Now, Alex was away that weekend and Thomas never took food or even drink without asking first, so Barry must have eaten six Hot Cross Buns in a 24-hour period. This in itself, although I thought greedy, didn't pose a problem for me; however, I did then suggest that as Thomas and I hadn't yet had a bun we should have the remaining two.

"No, it doesn't matter mum." Thomas piped up. "Dad can have it, I'm ok." This was typical of Thomas, as from a young child he had always been good at sharing and was respectful of his elders, but I wasn't having any of it!

"No, Thomas, it's fine, you can have one. I think Dad's had enough this weekend." I replied.

With that, Barry started shouting at Thomas, saying that he was disrespectful and should allow the adults to have the buns. I was amazed and started shouting back at him, "Barry, Thomas has just said you can have it. It's me who says you shouldn't. Don't have a go at him for it."

This didn't stop Barry, he carried on shouting abuse at Thomas, saying he was inconsiderate and even brought something totally irrelevant up, which had happened a couple of days earlier! Thomas wasn't arguing back, he just looked at Barry in amazement, wondering why he had reacted in this way.

I got the impression that Barry was taking the frustrations of our failing relationship out on Thomas, and it wasn't the first time. It was wrong and unjustified and made me see red. So much so that I flew into a wild rage, launching myself on Barry's lap and grabbing hold of his cheeks, to make him stop the tirade of abuse he was giving Thomas. Barry grabbed my arms and held them down by my sides, to calm me down, which I did very quickly, and then I asked him to let me go. At first he didn't let go, so I asked him again, at which point Thomas cried out in tears at the scene that was going on before him, "Dad let her go!" Barry released me and for a while afterwards I sat with Thomas cuddling and consoling him.

No more words were exchanged between Barry and I for the next two days. I had had enough. I could take a certain amount of flack, but when my son started to suffer because of it I would take no more. All my life, I have been a person that can endure a massive amount of discomfort for a relatively long time and will suffer in silence until something pushes me that little bit too far and then... pow! No more! If there was one thing that would push me over the edge, it was seeing my son suffer in any way whatsoever.

I couldn't find any possible reason for fighting to save our marriage anymore. Laurence had left home years before, and Alex no longer needed me to take care of him. Thomas didn't have a strong father/son relationship with his stepdad, so it made no odds if he was in the same house as him or not. Barry and I hadn't been happy together for years, if the truth were known.

As Barry and I sat in the office chatting two days later, I felt a huge amount of sadness. I cared about him very much, but I knew I didn't love him in the way a wife should love her husband.

"Barry," I said through tears of desperation, "we have both had our fair share of grief in our lives and we both deserve to be happy. And I don't think you are any happier than I am in this relationship. We mustn't fall out over this. We must be proud of ourselves and know that we supported each other and our boys through very challenging times. But now we must accept that it obviously was never meant to be forever."

That is honestly what I felt. For the 10 years that I had known Barry, I had had a job to do – to take care of him and his two sons – and now my job was done!

Chapter Forty-Two

We decided not to tell anyone, not even the boys, until we had had time to talk things through and get our heads around what in the end became a mutual decision. It wasn't a decision that Barry would have ever made, because ultimately his life was better for having me there; however, he knew that he would never be totally happy while I was unhappy.

The following weeks weren't easy. We slept in separate rooms without the boys noticing and tried to come to a conclusion regarding where we would live until the divorce was finalised. Barry refused to move out of the house, his main reason being that it was also his place of work, even though it was mine too! He questioned why we couldn't continue to live separate lives in the same house, but I knew this would not be a suitable option. It would be okay for him because nothing would change. I would continue to do all the shopping, cooking, washing and household chores for everyone.

I found myself wanting to go out with friends more because the alternative was spending the evening with him in the lounge. Every time I got dressed up to go out, he would question me as to where I was going and ask if it was with another man. I knew there was no way living in the same house would work, so I would just have to rent a place for Thomas and me until the financial aspects were settled. This would mean me finding another income to supplement the small amount I was getting from working in our own business to be able to afford the rent.

I contacted our friend, Charles, who owned a building company and asked if he needed a decorator. I had done plenty of painting and decorating throughout the years and thought I was quite good, but had only ever done jobs for myself or for family, never as paid work. Thankfully, he was able to give me work. I continued doing three days in our office and two days for him.

I really enjoyed my decorating work and had the same healthy fatigue at the end of each day as I had while working on my father's barn in France. My first job was to paint Charles's and his son Stewart's new home prior to them moving in. I worked alongside a man called John, who was not your normal builder-type and was a real gentleman with a kind heart. He would pop to the shops on the way to work to buy bread, cheese, olives and wine, which we would eat on the patio under the warm sun. It really was as close to working in France as I could get and I loved it!

Other tradesmen would regularly come and go to do work on the house, and on one occasion a man called Mark came to work on the lighting and sound system. I was up a ladder painting the ceiling when the doorbell rang so John went to answer it. As I looked round to say hello and introduce myself, my heart skipped a beat.

Standing there was what I thought was one of the most handsome men I had ever seen. Mark had dark hair, was not particularly tall, and was scruffily dressed in work clothes and white trainers (a pet hate of mine). But he had a smile that would make any woman's stomach do a somersault! When he smiled at me with his sparkling light blue eyes and his wide, white-toothed smile, I almost melted on the spot.

'Get a grip, woman!' I thought to myself. 'You're in no position to be falling for someone this soon after your marriage has ended.' Regardless of the fact that I had not had those types of feelings for Barry for a long time, I still knew the last thing I needed at that moment was another man in my life. I needed to be alone for a while, but that didn't stop the uncontrollable feeling I had in the pit of my stomach! Mark and I made small talk for a few minutes and I got the impression that, although he chatted very easily, he wasn't the most confident of people, which made him even more attractive to me. I also got the impression that he hadn't had the same initial reaction to me as I had had to him! Ah well, that was a good thing, I supposed! It didn't stop me hoping, as I went back to my work that our paths would cross again.

One day, John and I were chatting over lunch and he told me that Charles and Stewart were looking for people to go skiing with them in a couple of weeks' time. Stewart's godfather owned a chalet in the French Alps and every year Charles would book it for a week with the intention of filling it with whatever friends wanted to go. He had had some friends drop out at the last minute and needed to fill their places to get his money back, so John asked if Thomas and I would be interested in going along.

I was really excited about the prospect of doing this, as I'd always wanted to take Thomas skiing, but there was the big issue of how much it would cost me. I was trying to save to move out of my home with Barry and I knew that skiing wasn't cheap. John explained that it would cost a lot less than a normal ski trip, as we would be travelling by car with Charles and Stewart and the cost of the accommodation, once split between eight people, would be minimal.

Since my separation from Barry, I had a renewed vigour for life and was starting to remember what it was like to be the 'old' spontaneous, happy Alison, with nobody to hold me back or answer to. I felt free and had started to laugh and have fun in my life for the first time in years. I also got a huge amount of pleasure from being able to surprise and treat Thomas, who so deserved it.

"Blow it! Do you know what? Yes, we'll go!" I said excitedly to John. "As long as Charles and Stewart are okay with me taking Thomas."

They were okay with it. Charles had always commented on what a polite and well-behaved young man Thomas was. I drove home from work that night eager to give Thomas the news. He was obviously over the moon and very excited to be going skiing in just two weeks' time, during his Easter school holidays. Barry, on the other hand, was understandably not happy but knew there was nothing he could do about it.

A couple of days later, I discovered that Mark would also be joining the ski party. As neither Mark, Thomas nor I had been skiing before, we decided to have a couple of lessons at the dry ski slope in Folkestone. This also enabled Thomas and me to get to know Mark better before spending the week with him.

Chapter Forty-Three

We travelled in two cars to Les Arcs, a ski resort located in Savoie, France, in the Tarentaise Valley town of Bourg-Saint-Maurice. The chalet was beautiful and luxurious, with everything we could need for the week. It had a log burner and a massive verandah, which looked out over spectacular snowy, mountainous scenery.

Our party consisted of Charles, Stewart, John, Mark, Thomas, me, and Adele and Kev (a couple that Thomas, Mark and I met for the first time when we picked them up at the ferry port in Dover, at the start of our journey). Adele and I hit it off straight away. We were the same age and both had sons of similar ages; it was good to have another female in the house too!

We had all taken food and plenty of alcohol, and Charles and I had each prepared a couple of meals for the week, which would cut the cost of eating out. It turns out Mark was also a good singer and played guitar, so he had thrown his guitar in the boot of the car for good measure!

Most nights after skiing, we ate, drank, chatted, laughed, sang along to Mark's guitar playing and danced into the early hours; up until that time I don't think I had ever enjoyed myself that much in my life. Everyone got on well and we felt very relaxed in each other's company. It was an amazing week and one that I think started a metamorphosis in me. It made me realise that the years with Barry had aged me beyond my years and being with people nearer my own age again was good for me and so much fun! I felt alive again!

We partied well but still had time for skiing. Mark, Thomas and I would go off together, as we were the only learner skiers and were at the same level. Unfortunately, at Les Arcs there were no green runs so it was trial and error finding the easier blue runs. We would often have to stop for a rest and a long, cold drink, and it was during these times, when the others weren't around, that Thomas and I got to know Mark better. I found out that he was six years my senior and was born in East London, just a few miles down the road from where I was born. He, like me, had moved away from London when he was four or five years old. This probably explained why I found him so easy to be around; we were both Londoners!

During one of our après ski sessions, while Thomas was skiing on the low slopes nearby, I asked him about his private life as I felt that we knew each other well enough for me to broach the subject. He explained that he had been married twice before. Both wives had ended the marriage, which had devastated him, as in both instances they had a young family. He couldn't understand why someone would want to break a family up in that way. The one saving grace was that he had continued to have his two youngest sons, from his second marriage, to stay every weekend in the years since the breakup. However, he still found it very hard during the week not seeing them and going home to an empty house.

He then went on to tell me that a relationship he had been in had recently ended. Although he had only been seeing the girl for three months, he was besotted with her and was struggling to get over her ending it. I say 'girl' because she was 19 years his junior, which made me think back to when I first met him and my fleeting thoughts of getting to know him better. After hearing that his second wife and his girlfriend were much younger than him, I realised I wasn't his type, especially as I was much older than my years!

All in all, I found Mark to be a very kind, compassionate man who not only listened and cared but was also very good with Thomas, keeping an eye out for him on the ski slopes and always finding something to talk to him and laugh about. If nothing else, I would be happy to continue to have Mark as a good friend in our lives.

On the last day of skiing, when Mark had gone off to get him, me and Thomas a drink, Thomas made a very unusual comment to me. It was a comment that I would not have expected him to say at 13 years old; at the time, I found it odd that he would make a point of saying it.

"Mark's a really nice man isn't he? I like him a lot!"

"Yes, he is Thomas. That's really weird that you should say that because I was just thinking how very alike Daddy he is in many ways."

Chapter Forty-Four

After returning from our holiday, we adults continued to socialise as a group on the odd occasion and I found this light relief from being in the house with Barry. It gave me something to look forward to and meant I could continue with the fun and laughter I had got used to having again.

Eventually, in the June I found somewhere in Dover for Thomas and me to live, albeit temporarily until the divorce went through and I could buy us a house. I had to completely furnish our new home, as Barry needed every bit of furniture we owned. Thankfully, I was able to take many kitchen items with me as he wasn't a cook and would never use them; I did, of course, leave him the microwave. It was something I could live without and he couldn't.

I had to beg, steal and borrow, as the saying goes. I was given some third-hand bunk beds by a friend of my sister's, one for Thomas to sleep in, and the other as a spare for when family visited. I managed to find a second-hand, wooden bedframe for me, and a bar table and two stools from the Heart Foundation shop. The bar table and stools only cost me £60, and would do until such a time as I could afford a proper dining room table and chairs.

For six weeks we had no comfortable seating for the

lounge and sat on beanbags and deckchairs. Eventually, I realised that I may as well buy some new sofas, as we would need them when we bought a house anyway, so I bought them through the Next catalogue, which meant I could pay for them over a number of months. Unfortunately, there were many other necessities I couldn't afford to buy with cash and had to put on my credit card. This wasn't a good start, but I hoped that the divorce would go through quickly, enabling me to pay off my growing debts.

I managed to make the place very homely, and Thomas and I both loved coming home to it every day. Thomas seemed to change too, appearing brighter and happier. It was as if he knew he had his happy, cheerful, carefree, positive and fun 'Mumma' back, and that's all he needed. He also had friends living within walking distance, which meant they could come to us after school or he could go to them.

I felt almost elated at my newfound 'freedom'. It had been almost nine years to the day since Barry, the boys and I had moved into our own home together, and now it was just Thomas and me... again! I had fought harder in the previous nine years than I had ever fought in my life, and I didn't want to fight anymore. Life had become simple once more. I loved having visitors and soon after we had moved in my sister, my niece and a friend came to stay with us for a weekend. We all enjoyed some much-needed girlie time together.

I bought Thomas a budgie, which he had constantly nagged me for for years but hadn't been able to have, as Barry had been allergic to feathers. He named him Charlie and spent hours playing with him and training him to do tricks. We even started to have a fairly regular dinner guest during the weeks in the form of Mark! I think he enjoyed having someone to talk to at the end of his working day and although I had Thomas as company, I will admit that it was good to have some adult company to share my day with. Sometimes, if Mark and I had a couple of drinks, Mark would stay and sleep in the spare room. There were times that he just couldn't face going home to an empty house and he enjoyed the family atmosphere at our home.

Although I loved having Mark visit us, it was becoming more and more difficult for me. I was finding it hard to control my growing fondest for him, which wasn't reciprocated. On one occasion, as Mark left to go home, I spontaneously blurted out that I was going to miss him until the next time I saw him. My comment seemed to make him very uncomfortable and he couldn't wait to get out of the door.

Feeling bad for causing him obvious discomfort, I sent him a text as soon as he left, apologising for making my feelings known and for any embarrassment I had caused him. The wait until he got home and read my text seemed to go on forever, and I lay in bed awaiting his reply, which did eventually come but wasn't what I wanted to read.

He wrote, "I'm sorry but I just don't feel that way about you and am not ready for another relationship."

Well, to say I was devastated was an understatement. I felt bereft and cried myself to sleep that night. I was amazed at the strong emotions his text had invoked in me, and I remember thinking that I hadn't felt this bad since losing Tony. So this was what unrequited love felt like. It was the first time I had experienced it and I didn't like it one bit!

Chapter Forty-Five

After that day, I decided to back off from seeing Mark for a while, as I couldn't cope with the utter agony of knowing that he didn't want me like I wanted him. Whenever I was with him, it was all I could do to not pull him close to me and nuzzle the soft, warm, fresh-smelling soft skin of his neck.

I was often being asked out for a drink or dinner by other single men that I knew and started to accept the odd invitation, in the hope that it would take my mind off Mark, but it never really did. None of them made me feel as good as when I was with him. There was one man that I did become very fond of, and he of me, but distance was an issue and we realised that a relationship at this point in our lives, with the added responsibility of children, would be too difficult, so we ended it before it really got going.

However, Mark continued to contact me, asking me out for a drink or dinner or texting to ask if he could pop in on his way home from work as he was in the vicinity. This would inevitably end in him staying for dinner. My heart always missed a beat whenever I got a text from him and I felt that he was being cruel by not letting me move on. I just didn't get him. He was playing with my emotions, letting me know in no uncertain terms that he didn't want a relationship with me but appearing to not be able to live without seeing me for more than a few days! Or did he just prefer my cooking to his? He also still went out on occasions with his ex-girlfriend, which I felt was not helping him to get over her and move on, but he had to do what he had to do.

He even invited me to meet his family, and I often went to clubs with them, where they would all get up on stage and sing. The first time I heard Mark sing Elton John's 'Don't Let the Sun Go Down on Me', I got goose bumps and cried. Not only did he sing it extremely well, but it also brought back wonderful memories of Tony, and the day he and I had danced in the middle of Wembley Stadium as Elton John sung while the sun went down.

From the moment I met Mark's father, Les, and the rest of his family, I felt so welcome. They were just like the type of people I had grown up with, all Londoners and such lovely, happy, friendly folk to spend time with. Feeling so comfortable with his family made it even harder for me to accept that there would be no relationship between Mark and me; it all seemed so perfect, and I already felt like part of his family.

I knew that I could decline his invites or ignore his texts, but that was just too hard for me to do! I suppose that's one of the down sides to being a positive person: I have always believed that the impossible is possible and have always had hope! I suppose the other reason for accepting his invites was that he was a great support and friend to me during the time after I separated from Barry. Although life felt much easier for me, I continued to face many challenges and these were made more bearable by having a good, kind person around.

By the November of that year, the decorating work eventually came to an end. I was extremely grateful to Charles for giving me work, but I felt that, in the end, he was trying to find jobs for me to do in order to help me out and he shouldn't have had to do that. I didn't want to put him in the awkward position of having to tell me he no longer needed my services. So, when the old friend, who had lived with Barry and me for six months, with his family, offered me work, I accepted. The friend was a solicitor with his own law practice and I had been doing the odd bit of unpaid administrative work for him, just to help him out. He offered me full-time work as, by this time, Barry had 'let me go' from our own business.

I was slightly concerned at accepting a full-time position with him because he had told me that money was a bit tight at that time, which was why I had agreed to work for him for free in the first place. However, I had no choice. I needed work to pay the rent and bills and there was nothing else on offer at the time. So I became a paralegal of sorts, which after my compliance training came quite easily to me. I really enjoyed the work and threw myself into learning all I could. I worked alongside another lady who mainly worked on conveyancing and we became good friends.

My solicitor friend worked unusual hours compared to most solicitors I know, usually coming into the office around about lunchtime and working until late at night. This meant that although my hours were nine to five, I would often be there until late at night to complete the work that he assigned me when he came into the office later in the day.

After about five months of doing this, not only did I start

to become very tired, working for 12 hours each day in the office, but also Thomas became a 'latchkey kid', which filled me with tremendous guilt. He would get home from school around 4pm and be alone for five hours until I got home from work. So not only was I not there to feed him at a reasonable hour or to ensure he was doing his homework, but I also soon realised that he was spending hours playing computer games, which I had never allowed and had always been around to monitor. I couldn't blame him – he was a teenager and it was a natural thing for him to do – but I still didn't like it.

As I feared, it was touch and go each month as to whether my friend would have the funds to pay me, and in the May he actually didn't. I became more and more overdrawn in my bank as the rent and bills began to go out and eventually I plucked up the courage to ask him when I was going to get paid. When I told him I was overdrawn, his response was one of anger, saying that my debt was nothing like the ones he had.

Two days later, on the Saturday morning, I received a letter through the post from him. Enclosed was a cheque covering the previous month's salary and a letter 'firing' me! As I read the letter, my hands trembled. He had come up with a number of untruths, which he cited as the reasons for letting me go. He ended the letter by saying that, when he had sufficient funds, he would pay the £600 or so that he owed me for the hours I had done that month, and he enclosed a payslip for it! I never did receive this money.

I was distraught at the prospect of having no job and hence no money to pay the bills, but was mostly angry at this so-called 'friend', who I had helped out in his and his children's hour of need, for making false accusations about me so that he could fire me. I understood that he had to lay me off because he couldn't afford to pay me and that he wanted to protect his reputation as a solicitor, however, it could ruin the excellent reputation that I had worked years to build in one fell swoop!

I phoned my mother, hysterical and in floods of tears, and she arrived in no time at all to find me a blubbering wreck. She was worried sick, thinking that this would lead to me having a nervous breakdown, after my health had been so good for so long.

Chapter Forty-Six

It was at that point in my life that I knew I had recovered from ME, because that incident and a few more difficult times after that didn't lead to a relapse. After losing my job, I was unable to claim Jobseeker's Allowance as I had assets of over £19,000: the house that I had bought and which Barry was living in, which I received no income from. I had worked all my life from the age of 17, with only about a four-year break when Thomas was a baby and Tony was ill, and the first time I ever needed financial support I couldn't get it. Added to that, Thomas had no father around to help me out. Unable to pay the rent, I had to give up our home.

My mother's home in Dover wasn't big enough to house both Thomas and me comfortably, although she would have gladly had us there and we would have managed, of course. However, my friend, Una, welcomed Thomas and me into her home for as long as we needed and for this I will be forever grateful. Una was a widow whose family had all grown and flown the nest. She was rattling around in a three-storey, four-bedroomed house, so was glad of the company. Thomas and I took over the whole of her attic floor and were very comfortable indeed. I put all our furniture and possessions into storage, apart from the few bits we needed.

The only money Una asked of me was the difference she had to pay in Council Tax, due to no longer living alone, and we shared the cost of food. She was amazingly kind to us and her offer of accommodation meant that I didn't get any further into debt, since my annuity from Tony's pension was enough to pay for everything we needed, including the storage of our furniture.

I had immediately started to apply for jobs after losing my last one and within a few weeks I was asked to interview for an Office Administrator position at the Harvey Grammar School in Folkestone. The first stage of the interview process was a whole day, team affair, which was all very new to me. In fact, at the age of 43 I had never had a formal interview. Every job I ever got in the City was through knowing someone already or by chatting down the pub. After that, it was my Financial Adviser who gave me a job and then Barry and I set up our own business.

I really enjoyed the team interview day and thought that if I didn't get the job, at least I'd had practice and seen what was involved in going for a job these days. A few days later, I was over the moon to hear that I was one of the five finalists that had been asked back for the second part of the interview process.

I felt that the second interview went well and was told that I would be informed of their decision the following week. However, that evening I was upstairs with Thomas when Una shouted up to say there was a phone call for me. It was the Office Manager, Karen, calling to say that I had got the job and that she was pleased to say that the decision by the panel was unanimous! I felt both proud and relieved, and also ecstatic at the prospect of enjoying the summer holidays, knowing that I had a job to go to in the September.

A year prior to this, Una had asked me if I would go with her to her son Paul's wedding, which was being held in San Diego. Paul was marrying a lovely Californian girl, Mary, who I had met in the UK a few years before. How could I refuse? I felt very privileged to be asked and accepted straight away. Little did I know that at the time of going I would be living with Una. This made it all the more exciting in the lead up to our trip, as we were able to discuss outfits, arrange visas and make other travel arrangements.

I loved San Diego and Mary's family, all of whom made us feel so at home and very welcome. The wedding was a fabulous affair held at a large golf resort, where most of the guests stayed for the whole weekend. Of course, due to the reliability of the Californian sun, the wedding and reception were held outdoors surrounded by vineyards.

In the days after the wedding, we hired a car and got to do some sightseeing, visiting many places including Mission Beach and La Jolla, an affluent, hilly, seaside community within the city of San Diego, which occupies seven miles of curving coastline along the Pacific Ocean. We took a cruise around the Port of San Diego and did a wine tasting and ate lunch among the vines of the Wilson Creek Winery in the Temecula Wine Valley.

While we were away I had the odd text from Mark asking if I was having a good time. On one of the days I noticed a post by him on Facebook saying that he had been to hospital as he had cut the top of his thumb off. I felt sick and tried to ring him to find out how he was. When there was no reply I called his father, Les.

It was a relief to hear Les answer the phone. "'Ello babe! You okay?" he asked.

"Yes, I'm okay!" I replied. "But how's Mark? What's he gone and done?"

"Oh, 'e's okay now," Les explained. "The fool went and cut the top of his thumb with a circular saw, didn't 'e. Cut it right down to the bone 'e did. 'E's lost a bit of the tip but they've managed to stitch it up a bit. They gave 'im a tetanus, antibiotics and dressed it for 'im."

"Oh my God!" I said. "Poor Mark!"

"It's okay, though, luckily it's the only finger 'e doesn't use to play the guitar!" Les chuckled.

Later on, as I was getting ready for bed, I got a text from Mark saying that he was okay but in a lot of discomfort. I sent one back saying that I wished I could be there with him. I felt useless. He'd been there for me in the past year throughout all my problems, and then when he needed support I wasn't there for him; although, in a way, I HAD been there for him. I was often company and a listening ear at the end of his working day, someone for him to go out with. I had cooked his dinner on many occasions!

I got a text straight back saying, "I wish you were here too, babe!" and my heart skipped that familiar beat!

Chapter Forty-Seven

Three years later, and I am at a friend's wedding watching the other wedding guests in their revelry, and couples dancing together who are so obviously in love. I become distracted by the track that the DJ has begun to play, Celine Dion's 'The Reason'; it brings back a stream of memories and emotions, as music so often does with me. This was the song I played over and over again after Tony's death, and I would sing it at the top of my voice when the sobs would allow me to. This song, 'The Reason', and Thomas, 'my reason', kept me fighting on in my darkest days.

As I listen, I think back over the previous year. It had been a highly emotionally charged year for me, in which I was unusually very tearful. Tony was on my mind more than he had been for years. It started with Thomas passing his driving test just two months after his 17th birthday and driving his first car to school. Tony wasn't by my side to share in my pride as he drove off alone for the first time.

During that summer, we received the news that Thomas had passed the necessary A-levels and was accepted by the University of Greenwich to study for a degree in Fisheries Management. Again, Tony wasn't by my side to share in the immense pride that I felt in Thomas, not only at his achievement but also in the fact that he had chosen a subject that was his absolute passion, and for which his daddy had always had a strong love and fascination.

We also celebrated Thomas's 18th birthday that year by having a joint party for my grandmother's 90th birthday in our garden. It was a wonderful day with family, including Tony's mother and father, and old and new friends... but again, no Tony! As I watched my darling son enjoying his birthday, a handsome young man having fun and laughing, I couldn't help but think how proud his daddy would have been of him. I could also see that he was a real chip off the old block, very like Tony in lots of ways, and that is one of the many things I love about him.

Another big event that year was dropping Thomas and all his possessions off at university. It was one of the hardest days for me, and again Tony wasn't by my side! I hadn't really appreciated what 'empty nest syndrome' was until that previous month. I had been feeling very emotional in the weeks leading up to him leaving home, what with him turning 18 and the acceptance that he was no longer my little boy, but never believed that I would feel so much pain as I said goodbye to him and left him alone at his digs; my son and one true companion, who had looked after me since he was two years old.

I had held back my tears as I said goodbye because I knew he would worry about me, as he always did, but I cried for most of the drive home. What a weird feeling it was that suddenly my little boy, who had been my reason and who I had considered in every decision I made, was no longer with me and no longer needed me. I felt bereft and so lost but at the same time very proud at what he had achieved and the wonderful young man he had become.

So now, as I sit at my friend's wedding, a month after Thomas starting university, I smile to myself as I listen to the closing notes of Celine's song, marvelling at how far Thomas and I have come in the years since his daddy's death. All of a sudden, a familiar voice breaks into my reminiscing.

"So, do you think we should get married then?"

Unusually for me, I was speechless for quite a few seconds! Where on earth had that come from? I didn't even think he loved me in that way!

Years before, Mark had said that he would never marry again but I couldn't rid myself of the thought that maybe one day he would change his mind. Now, suddenly, here he was asking me to be with him for the rest of his life.

I smiled as I said, "Well we don't seem to be able to live without each other so..." I wasn't even sure at that moment whether he really meant it. He was, after all, only asking for my opinion on whether we should!

Our friendship had continued because, however hard we tried, we just couldn't seem to live without each other, and eventually we became much closer. To say we tested our relationship to the hilt would be a massive understatement, but that's a whole other story!

We eventually bought a house together because I knew I would rather be with him unmarried than not have him in my life at all! I loved our new home and I soon understood just how important having the right home, partner and home life is for your health. I had missed having a garden and this house, situated in a more rural area, had a beautiful, peaceful space in which to sit outside, and was surrounded by fields.

Mark, Thomas and I were very happy there.

After leaving Barry, I often thought that it probably wasn't just the relationship problems that made me unwell, but also the house and the environment I was in. I considered it very telling that in the years since my separation from Barry I never suffered a relapse of ME symptoms, even though I had endured many more stressful situations. Obviously, my continued changes in eating, exercise and mindset played a big part too!

Two friends came and joined us at our table and we started to chat about other things with them, but I found it very hard to concentrate on what they were saying. I couldn't believe how excited and happy Mark's question had made me, even if it was just a 'suggestion'! I thought it hadn't mattered to me that he didn't want to get married, but by the way my heart was pounding in my chest it obviously did!

In the four years that I had known him, I never felt that he really loved me, not in the way that he had loved his last girlfriend anyway. He had never shown feelings for me like the ones he had expressed about her, all those years ago when we were skiing.

I always felt that he settled into our relationship because he hated being on his own. He felt at ease with me, we shared the same interests, we were good friends, he loved my cooking, and all his needs were met... but maybe I was wrong, maybe he did feel a real love in his heart for me, as I always had for him!

As I got ready for bed that night, I was smiling like a Cheshire cat, which made him smile. The following morning Mark said, "So, I suppose you'll want a big wedding!"

"Oh no!" I replied, "I'd be happy to elope without telling a soul."

"Would you?" he sounded surprised.

"Do you not know me at all?" I said.

That day, I couldn't help but do a search on Google for places to get married. We didn't want to spend a fortune but thought it would be good to take the opportunity to have a holiday too, which we hadn't had for a while.

On the Sunday, I found an amazing deal and sent an email to The Wedding Travel Company, who were the ones offering it. The girl called me back that evening, but my mother was with us so I walked out of the room and asked the girl to call me back the next day. I'm sure my mother thought it suspicious, believing I was keeping something from Mark, not her.

The following day, while I was at work, the travel counsellor, Rachel, called me and we discussed the hotels we could have and the trips we could include. By the time I got home that night, I had a plan.

As we sat at the table eating fish and chips and drinking beer, Mark asked if I'd booked our wedding and honeymoon.

"No!" I replied. "You haven't asked me to marry you yet!"

"I did!" he said. "On Friday night!"

"No you didn't. You just said 'Do you think we should get married?' That's not a proposal!"

He looked at me, grinned and carried on eating his dinner. About 20 minutes later he said, "So, will you marry me then?"

"Sorry?" I said jokingly. "What did you say?" I just needed to hear him say it twice to make sure!

"Will you marry me?" he repeated.

I replied, "Yes, I would love to!" as I gave him a greasy-lipped kiss.

Some may say it was not the most romantic of marriage proposals, but for me it was just perfect and I felt ecstatic... finally... he loves me! I always knew he did; he just didn't know it himself!

Chapter Forty-Eight

Just four months later we were heading for a hotel at Gatwick Airport, feeling excited as well as naughty at the thought of running off to get married without anyone knowing. All that we told the family was that we were going on holiday to Las Vegas and New York.

The preparations for our wedding and honeymoon had been totally stress-free. Within a week I had booked with The Wedding Travel Company and they took care of everything from there, including all the travel bookings and the legal documents for the marriage. All we had to do was supply them with some information and sort out our outfits and rings... easy!

In my state of constant excitement since Mark's proposal, I found it really hard not to blurt everything out to family and friends. I have to say that Mark and I did tell a few people, but they were complete strangers that we met while in Prague or in shops or at the airport. The people we knew didn't even know that we had become engaged. Although Mark had a ring made for me, I didn't wear it because we were sure they would have guessed that we were going away to get married.

Thomas was the one I wanted to share the news with more than anything. In a way, I was glad that he was away at university because it meant I didn't have to tell him any white lies or try to hide things from him. The thought of our impending marriage and travel plans had taken my mind off my empty nest syndrome too!

We stayed at the Gatwick Manor hotel the night before our flight and as soon as we had checked in we went to the restaurant to have dinner. We made a toast to us and Mark slipped the ring on my finger.

During the night, I had trouble sleeping and was browsing Facebook when I came across a post from our friend, James, which said that his case was packed ready for his trip to Vegas. Although it was about four in the morning, I posted a comment asking when he was going and then drifted off to sleep. When I woke up I checked Facebook and James had replied... he was on the 11.20 flight, the same one as us!

We met up with James at the airport before going for breakfast and told him our news, but we swore him to secrecy and told him there should be no Facebook posts; we knew we could trust him. While chatting to him again on the plane, we arranged to meet him and his friends for a drink on the evening of our wedding.

At 2.30pm local time, Mark and I checked into a fabulous suite at the Luxor Hotel. The Egyptian-themed casino resort, on the south end of the Strip, is housed in a 30-storey pyramid, topped with a 315,000-watt light beam. We had a Tower Deluxe King room in one of the two towers attached to the pyramid and it was extremely comfortable and very high up. It overlooked both Frank Sinatra Drive and Dean Martin Drive and offered amazing views of the desert in the distance.

We went straight out to explore the various themed hotels and casinos on the Strip, walking for miles as the place was so vast. In the evening we ate Chinese food in a restaurant just off the Strip before venturing back to our hotel for some much-needed sleep.

The following day, we ate breakfast in the hotel next to ours, the Mandalay Bay. It was a buffet-style breakfast, with absolutely every type of food you could think of from all around the world, and included dishes suitable for breakfast, lunch and dinner. This was for the benefit of those who spent all their time in the casinos and lost track of what their next meal was.

We did some more exploring around the many hotels, including the Venetian, the Cosmopolitan, Caesar's Palace and the Bellagio, where we stood mesmerised by the Fountains of Bellagio, the most ambitious, choreographically complex water feature ever conceived. As it was early February the weather was spring-like, which meant we were in T-shirts and flip-flops but sometimes needed a light jacket.

There was just so much to take in and we walked miles. It's really difficult to judge the distance from one hotel to another along the Strip due to the vast size of the buildings and roads. On numerous occasions we would say "Oh let's just go over there!" and 'over there' would take half an hour to get to!

That evening, for our hen and stag parties, we went to see a show in our hotel. I can't recollect the name of it but it wasn't the best choice and Mark and I struggled to stay awake, partly because it was boring and also due to jet lag. We headed straight to bed afterwards, as we needed to be fresh and wide-awake for our wedding the following day.

Chapter Forty-Nine

The first thing I saw as I opened my eyes on the day of our wedding was my handsome husband-to-be. He was still snoozing and I couldn't resist snuggling up to his warm body and planting a soft kiss on his shoulder. As I did this he stirred, looked round at me, gave me one of his breathtakingly beautiful smiles, and said, "Morning babe!" I felt that oh-so-frequent flip in my stomach at the sight of his smile and kissed him passionately on the lips.

We had ordered room service for breakfast but had plenty of time to lie there in each other's arms while watching the sun rise over the desert. What an absolutely perfect start to our special day! We ate a very sweet, calorie-laden breakfast of pancakes, waffles, bacon and maple syrup and there was, as always in the States, far too much for the two of us! We both showered and I slipped on one of Mark's shirts, at which point a beautiful red rose posy was delivered for me, as well as a rose corsage for Mark.

Two friendly, young Californian girls came to our suite at about 10am to fix my hair and makeup and in the short time that they were there Mark sat watching them work their magic on me, while chatting to us and playing Candy Crush on his iPad.

"This is the most stress-free wedding day I've ever had!" he laughed as he lounged on the sofa.

I told the girls that we were really struggling with jetlag and that I didn't want to feel dozy on my wedding day.

"Ah, you need a vodka Red Bull!" one of them chipped in.

"But I don't like Red Bull," I said. "It makes me feel crazy and out of control."

"Ah, no! That's why you have it with vodka," she replied. "The Red Bull's an upper and the vodka's a downer! Balances it out, see!"

The girls did a wonderful job with my hair and makeup, and once they'd left Mark and I got dressed in all our finery and decided to go down to the bar to get a drink before our car came to collect us. It was the first time Mark had seen my wedding dress, which was actually just an ivory satin one-shoulder evening dress: long, straight and very simple, but elegant. With it, I wore tomato-red, suede, pointed stiletto shoes with an ankle strap and a wrap in the same colour for my shoulders. I also had a red, beaded clutch bag large enough to accommodate my lipstick as well as our mobile phones and passports.

Mark wore his slightly shiny, dark silver grey suit with a white shirt, red cravat, red waistcoat and shiny black shoes, and as always he looked gorgeous! My stomach did a somersault as he gave me one of his beaming smiles; this man was soon to become my husband and I couldn't have been happier.

As we walked through the hotel foyer and casino to the bar, many people congratulated us. They must see so many people get married out there all the time, but they still managed to make us feel special. At the bar we were given our vodka Red Bulls for free, which I have to say really did do the job.

We both visited the bathroom before heading off to find our chauffeur, and as we were travelling down the escalator from the bar, I felt my garter sliding down my leg. When we reached the bottom I nudged Mark and pointed to the floor at the same time as flicking my garter off the toe of my shoe. Mark, without hesitation and in one fell swoop, bent down, picked up the garter and put it in his pocket. What teamwork... I knew at that point just why I was marrying him!

Outside waiting for us was a shiny, white stretch limousine with a sign in the window saying 'Smith Wedding'. "That's us!" I said to Mark as we walked up to the chauffeur, who was dressed smartly in a grey suit, black waistcoat and black cap.

"Hi guys! How are you today? You ready to get married?" he said in his Californian drawl. He introduced himself as Chad and explained how our day would pan out. As he opened the door to let us in the car he explained that there was a bottle of champagne in the chiller that we could help ourselves to.

We were going to be married at the Valley of Fire State Park, located 50 miles (80km) northeast of Las Vegas, the oldest state park in Nevada, USA. It was designated as a National Natural Landmark in 1968 and covers an area of almost 42,000 acres (17,000ha). Its name is derived from red sandstone formations, the Aztec Sandstone, which formed from great shifting sand dunes during the age of the dinosaurs. These features, which are the centrepiece of the park's attractions, often appear to be on fire when reflecting the sun's rays. The rough floor and jagged walls of the park contain brilliant formations of eroded sandstone and sand dunes that are more than 150 million years old.

From the Strip we were going to head west on the Valley of Fire Highway through the Moapa Indian Reservation from Interstate 15 to the west, but before that we had a few legalities to complete. First of all, Chad drove up to a little white chapel where he competed some paperwork and collected the cash that we would use to pay for our marriage licence. He then drove a little further and dropped us off outside the Clark County Court House where we had to complete all the legal paperwork.

It was all so surreal and as we got back in the car to continue the hour-long journey to the Valley of Fire, we giggled like a couple of teenagers at the thought of our families back home, oblivious to the big commitment we were about to make to each other. The further we got away from Las Vegas, the more barren the scenery became, but when we neared the Valley of Fire the colour of the rocks started to change from a sandy colour to a deep red. It was so beautiful.

When we got out of the car we immediately felt the warm sun on our heads. The sight of the massive, flame-red rock formations against the deep blue, cloudless sky was quite breath taking and Mark and I felt completely satisfied with our decision to marry there. We chatted with the photographer for a while, who was not only going to be taking professional photos of us but was also recording video of our marriage ceremony. Shortly after that, the pastor arrived to conduct our service. She was a typical Californian-looking lady: slim and attractive with long blonde hair, she was dressed in a black top and black trousers.

The service was short but perfect and I remember thinking how very different it was, not having to think about members of the congregation looking on. We were totally together as one, not having to think about anyone or anything else. The words we said to each other were for us and us alone and in a way felt more real. We both felt emotional as we said our vows to each other. When the pastor pronounced us husband and wife, we kissed each other hard on the lips. I was so happy to become Mark's wife and knew that this one was for keeps!

Unlike a traditional church wedding, our photo session involved me hitching up my long dress to climb the rocks and make the most of the amazing scenery. We wondered how brides who got married in the middle of the summer managed with the heat, as even in February I started to perspire out there in the desert. We were grateful to get back into our air-conditioned limo and have our champagne.

At about 4pm, Chad dropped us off at the venue I had booked for our wedding supper and before leaving us he gave us another bottle of champagne, two engraved champagne flutes and a wedding cake. We thanked him for his wonderful care and attention and then walked through the casino of the Stratosphere Hotel, where we took a lift up to the Top of the World restaurant, 800 feet above the Las Vegas Strip.

We ate delicious gourmet food and drank cocktails in the revolving restaurant as we watched the sun go down on our day, which seemed appropriate, as we had watched the sun come up together that morning. Later, we took a taxi back to our hotel, changed out of our wedding gear and went to meet our friend, James, and his friend, Les, for a couple of drinks. However, we didn't stay long as we had a very important job to do; there was the small matter of breaking the news to our families.

In the days before we left home, I told Thomas that I would FaceTime him so that I could show him the scenery from our hotel suite. I arranged a day and a time with him to make sure he was in his room and near a Wi-Fi connection. The time I arranged was midnight our time, which would be 8am his time. I wanted and needed him to be the very first person to hear our news and wanted to tell him to his face.

Mark and I sat on the sofa in our suite and I nervously dialled his number using FaceTime, but the call wouldn't connect. I tried again but there was still no joy, so I sent him a text asking him if he was in a Wi-Fi area. His reply was "Oh, sorry Mum, I'm on the riverbank fishing and I don't have Wi-Fi!" This really made me laugh. I thought, 'That's just typical there's me trying to tell him his mum's got married again and he's fishing!'

As we wanted to tell everyone else before they went to work or went out for the day, we needed to tell them before we went to bed, so I decided to ring Thomas and tell him on the phone, putting him on loudspeaker so that Mark could hear.

"Hi sweetheart! I've got something to tell you. Mark and I got married today."

"Oh wow! That's brilliant! Congratulations! I don't believe it you sneaky pair! I'm so happy for you both."

"Thanks mate!" Mark piped in.

I never had any doubt that Thomas wouldn't be upset by the way we did it and that we hadn't told him beforehand. I knew that he would almost be embarrassed by me having a big wedding with lots of guests at my age. He didn't like being in the limelight himself, and I wouldn't put it past him if he wanted to get married in this way when his time came. I also knew just how much he had always thought of Mark, and that Mark had been the closest thing to a father that he'd had since Tony died.

Not long after putting the phone down to him, I received a text saying, "Love you Mummy! So proud of you!" That was all I needed and all I cared about.

We rang, Skyped and sent texts to the rest of our close family, who were all elated by the news, and before going to bed I posted a photo of us at the Valley of Fire in our wedding outfits and a photo of our marriage certificate on Facebook, without any comment.

The next morning, we awoke to more than 60 comments on my Facebook post from friends and family, all congratulating us and sending their best wishes; there were also many comments about our sneakiness, of course! We were really grateful to have had Facebook, as these comments were like wedding greeting cards and made us feel like our family and friends were with us after all. The comments continued to come in over the following days and we enjoyed reading every one of them.

That day, we went on a helicopter trip to the Grand Canyon, which was something I had always wanted to do. We then took photos under the famous Las Vegas sign.

Chapter Fifty

Early the following morning, we took a flight to New York, where we spent the last five days of our honeymoon. We were greeted by thick snow and temperatures well into the minuses. Thankfully, we had gone prepared with thermals. Having been to New York in the winter before, I knew how bitterly cold it could get.

We saw many of the famous sights and Mark was delighted when he saw on the news that we were out there at the same time as the 50th anniversary of The Beatles' appearance on *The Ed Sullivan Show*. There was lots of coverage on TV and we were able to get photos of CBS Studios, which had been decorated in commemoration of the event.

I was amazed and moved by what had been built at the Ground Zero site since the last time I had visited a year after the 9/11 attacks; all I saw then was the leftover rubble and crumbled wreckage of the twin towers, along with flowers and messages from loved ones tied to the metal fencing around the site. Now there is the magnificent new Tower 1, memorial fountains, a museum and the Tree of Life, also known as the Survivor Tree.

We visited the top of The Empire State Building at night during a snowstorm, which was so beautiful and very romantic, and it also happened to be a couple of days before Valentine's Day!

We took a train from Penn Station out to Metuchen in New Jersey to visit our dear friends Jim and Maria. Jim was the American attorney that my father met through business, years prior and he and his family later became good family friends. The last time Mark and I saw Jim and Maria was when they were visiting Paris and we decided to take the Eurostar over to meet them for dinner.

As I got off the train and stepped onto the snowy platform at Metuchen, I heard someone shout, "Here she is, here comes the bride!" and as I looked around I saw Jim, wrapped up against the cold, standing at the other end of the platform. He rushed over to us and gave me a big hug. "That's from me, and this one's from your dad," he said. He had Skyped my father in France that morning and my father had joked about Jim getting to see his newly married daughter before him.

Maria cooked us a delicious beef Sunday lunch with a starter of mussels and a dessert of little buns that she had made and iced with 'Mark', 'Alison' and 'Just Married'. We had a very enjoyable time with them and two of their friends and left later that evening to get the train back to New York, laden with leftover food that Maria packed in a bag for us.

On the day we were due to fly home we took a long walk through Central Park, which looked just like a winter wonderland, with its thick coating of snow and The Jackie Onassis Lake completely frozen over. We were sad to say goodbye to New York and the amazing suite we had on the top floor of the New Yorker Hotel in mid-town Manhattan, just a stone's throw from Madison Square Garden. The bedroom of our suite was on the corner of the building with double-aspect views, one of which was The Empire State Building in all its glory, seen from the comfort of our bed.

On the journey home I reflected on the previous 10 days. It amused me that we had spent most of our time away in high places – up in the sky on planes, in a suite at the top of the Luxor Hotel, at the top of the Stratosphere Hotel, in a helicopter over the Grand Canyon, sitting high up on the edge of the rocks looking down into the Grand Canyon, at the top of The Empire State Building, on the top floor of the New Yorker Hotel. And now here I was, going home a very happy Mrs Smith and feeling on top of the world!

Like the water bug in Doris Stickney's book, there had been many times in my life when I didn't know where I was going, I didn't know what the future had in store and I was scared of what was beyond each day. But now I felt different. I felt alive and full of joy for what my life had in store, and nothing scared me. At last, I could feel grateful for the challenges of my past, which had enabled me to evolve and to not sweat the small stuff. I had become just like that beautiful dragonfly, dancing on the water of life.

THE END
(Or is it the beginning?)

Epilogue

One thing that my life so far has taught me is that taking responsibility for our own lives, our health, our lifestyle and our thoughts is paramount to our wellbeing. We all have those flight or fight times in our lives and it is entirely our own decision as to what we choose to do.

I know I would never have totally recovered from ME or been able to be the happy, positive and healthy person I am today without putting in the work and looking after 'me' first. I decided to share my story with others in the hope that it would give those who needed and wanted it the inspiration to carry on through the challenging times in their lives.

Thankfully, I knew from the start that taking the medication prescribed by my GP to treat my symptoms was absolutely the last thing my body needed. Although it was a struggle to endure the pain and depression for a long time, without the quick fix of pain killers or anti-depressants, I knew that I had to get through it by treating the root cause of these problems by natural means, which doesn't happen overnight.

There is an amazing amount of help, support and guidance out there, in the form of therapists and experts; we just need to accept it, learn from it, implement the knowledge and do whatever it takes to improve our lives and grow.

Why oh why, when medical professionals tell someone with ME/CFS or burnout that there is nothing they can do to help them, don't they advise them to try holistic therapies? Unfortunately, I think we all know the answer to that, but that's a whole other debate!

During my recovery years, I discovered and used many beneficial therapies, including reiki, aromatherapy, reflexology, Indian head massage, Jin Shin Jyutsu, acupuncture, neuro linguistic programming (NLP), hypnotherapy, Emotional Freedom Technique (EFT) and colonic hydrotherapy, some of which I later trained in and qualified to practice in. All of these had a beneficial effect on my health in one way or another; however, I think it comes down to preference as to which therapies people choose and are most comfortable with. I also visited naturopaths and nutritionists to discover which foods were having a negative impact on my health and to find out which nutritional supplements could support my health and healing.

Years after recovering from ME, I discovered Sophrology. Sophrology, described by its founder as a philosophy, a way of life, a therapy and a personal development technique, was created in Spain in 1960 and is extremely popular in continental Europe. Sophrology seems to cover many of the areas that it took me years to discover and start implementing; I wish I'd known about it years ago when I was working in London and suffering from regular bouts of burnout.

It's about time school children were taught these kinds of preventative self-help therapies, as well as the importance of good nutrition and having the right mindset. This may just reduce many of the increasingly common health problems that we are seeing in adulthood, which are putting a strain on our health services.

My belief is that some people are more prone to burnout, ME and other similar conditions than others. Whether it's their genetic make-up, their personality traits, their beliefs or just the way they live their life, I don't know and actually to me it doesn't matter; they are suffering and need to get better. Surely that's all that matters!

Through research, I have found that too many sufferers are spending any precious energy they have on trying to figure out why they are ill, or campaigning for medical professionals to find a reason for their suffering. Even if they did find a reason, they would probably only throw prescribed medication at the symptoms. Sufferers need to be using their energy to work on improving their health naturally; there is no quick fix. What is needed is a good dose of belief, taking responsibility and determination.

I also noticed that there are far more support groups out there that 'support' sufferers to endure the condition than ones that teach them how to move forward and improve their lives. This only reinforces what the medical professionals tell them; that there is no cure. Well, I am the proof that there is one.

This makes me even more passionate about sharing the knowledge that I have gained in my life with those who are willing to do whatever it takes to better their health and their lives. A good place to start, if you want to know how I did it, is my website, www.justalison.me

Within a period of about four or five years, I transitioned

to a completely new way of living and being. I am grateful everyday for everything I have, and for what I have endured, and I never think about the things I don't have. Even though life has thrown, and will continue to throw, more curveballs at me, I know that my newfound knowledge, mindset and habits will never lead me back to ME!

In Memory of

my truly amazing, late husband, Tony (1955 – 1997)
and
my dear, departed Grandad, Bill. (1922 – 2012)

Without both of them there would be no story and I wouldn't have everything that I'm so grateful for today.

Acknowledgements

I wish to express my gratitude to all the individuals and companies who contributed to the production of this book, but special thanks go to:

Mark - without your tireless encouragement and support I would probably never have completed this book. You believed in me, even when I didn't believe in myself, and kept your patience with me throughout the whole formatting process! The hours spent, and amazing work you put in, on the cover text are very much appreciated. I will be forever grateful that you gave me the opportunity to step off the treadmill, enabling me to breathe properly again and to follow my dreams. Together we are stronger and I love you with all my heart!

Mum and Dad - where would I be without your constant, unfaltering love and support through my good times and my bad? Not once have you judged me, allowing me to make my mistakes but always being by my side when I had to live with the fallout. I am grateful for the life and the unconditional love you have both given me! I love you so much and I thank you for making my life such a rewarding one.

Nan - thank you for being a huge inspiration in my life and for helping towards making my book the best quality it could be; the story of special people deserves special treatment and

I only wish that Grandad were still with us to read it.

Isabel Frewer – I can't thank you enough for the amazingly beautiful illustration you created for the cover of my book. You listened intently to my wishes, understood them perfectly and got it so right...thank you!

Lizzie Ferrar and Rachael Grant at Proofreading London - your help, advice, support and professional, speedy service has been invaluable, thank you!

Jeremy Cowley – I am delighted that you didn't just cast your professional eye over my manuscript but quite unexpectedly read it from cover to cover...and enjoyed it! Thank you for all your valuable advice and feedback.

References

Recommended reading:

- The Secret by Rhonda Byrne
- You Can Heal Your Life by Louise L. Hay
- Instant Serenity for Life and Work – An Introduction to Sophrology by Florence Parot
- NLP Workbook by Joseph O'Connor

For excellent Proofreaders see www.proofreadinglondon.com

To be kept up-to-date with my blogs, workshops, webinars and future books, please go to www.justalison.me to register for updates.

Please stay connected at www.facebook.com/justalison.me/

If you enjoyed reading my book I would love to know, please tweet me on @JustAlisonMe with the bits you liked best, adding #myreasonandme